COUNTY ROADS

D1501106

Around Ontario with
Global Television's

TERRY CULBERT

GSPH

Published by

GSPH GENERAL STORE
      PUBLISHING HOUSE

1 Main Street, Burnstown, Ontario, Canada K0J 1G0
Telephone 1-800-465-6072 Fax (613) 432-7184

ISBN 1-896182-21-6
Printed and bound in Canada

Layout and Design by Leanne Enright
All photos and cartoons are by the author unless otherwise indicated.

Front cover photo by Sjoerd Witteveen
The author is holding a five-week-old Romanov-Dorset cross fall-born lamb on the
farm of Dana and Joanne Vader in Cherry Valley, Prince Edward County.

General Store Publishing House gratefully acknowledges the assistance of the
Ontario Arts Council and Canada Council.

Canadian Cataloguing in Publication Data

Culbert, Terry, 1942-
    Terry Culbert's county roads

ISBN 1-896182-21-6

    1. Ontario--Description and travel--1981-
I. Title

FC3077.1.A1C84 1995   917.13   C95-900433-5
F1056.8.C84 1995

First Printing July 1995

For Donna-Marie

ACKNOWLEDGEMENTS

There are a lot of people who give you support in one form or another when you're doing a big project like this. I'd like to thank Ian Bowering, curator of Inverarden Regency Cottage Museum in Cornwall, for looking at my mock-up draft and seeing the potential of a book. Ian also was instrumental in introducing me to the wonderful people at the General Store Publishing House in Burnstown, Ontario. Publisher Tim Gordon, his assistant Rosemary Nugent, art director Leanne Enright and the entire staff have been a tremendous help to me as I prepared my first book. John Stevens of Toronto was the man given the task of editing my stories. The author/editor has been most kind to me the first time out. In a world of computers, fax machines and 800 numbers, the fact that I live in southern Ontario and General Store Publishing House is in the Ottawa Valley near Renfrew means nothing. In a high-tech world they're as close as next door.

At Global Television, I'm grateful to producer Larry Jackson. He took me under his wing at the beginning of 1994, spending a lot of time helping me improve my scriptwriting. This book would not have been possible if it weren't for the likes of Larry giving me story ideas which, when completed, were used on his *News at Noon*. Producer Mark Trueman, son of the former Global anchorman Peter Trueman, has been very supportive and uses my stories regularly on his weekend newscasts. Anchormen Robert Fisher and Peter Kent are forever supplying me with story leads. Producers Ron Waksman, Ian Blair, John Arntzen and Bonnie Laufer-Krebs have all used my stories on their various shows. One group that I regard as being very special are the editors: supervisor Fred Groten, Doug McLellan, Vince Robinet, Jerry Cascone, Tom Boldt, George Gedeon, Tony Wilde, Jim Wenger, Joe Da Ponte, Julie Clark and Vicki Ryznar-Anderson. This team of tape editors have put up with me for years and have always made assembling my stories for air a pleasurable experience. Inga Belge, Sharon Murphy and Cal Johnston on the assignment desk have been marvellous, giving me a lot of freedom. To David O'Rourke, Manager of Production Administration and Finance, and Sandy Ciebleman, Rosie Corbett, and Dorothy Skiba, for keeping me in pocket money as I travelled the province; to the library staff for finding historic footage or music when I required it; to Reg Thomas, Executive Producer of News, and Gail Mugford my supervisor, both for being supportive; to director Terry Lewis, who knows and loves this province as I do; to Jackie Feig on reception. She not only keeps tabs on me but passes story tips my way as well; to David Hamilton, Director of

Public Relations, for all his encouragement; to ENG maintenance under supervisor Fred Merrimen and his team including Ilkka Ahola, Chris Bott and Lou Pirocchi; and to the dozens of people behind the scenes that make it possible for my stories to be shown to all of you . . . I say thanks.

To my two sisters, Dana Garrett in London and Mary Jane Culbert at *Maclean's* magazine in Toronto, thanks for your newspaper clipping service. Thanks also to neice Heather Brennan of Kingston for teaching this blockhead the proper way to get in and out of his computer; to poor little Holly, the youngest of our dogs. She would become so upset with the sound of the three-hole punch as I assembled my manuscript, that I was forced to go out to the car and close the door so that she wouldn't hear the squeak. At night, during the winter, I'd have to bundle up and trudge outside, turn on the interior light, then punch away; and to my wife Donna who has put up with me working on this project for over a year. You should have seen the expression on her face when I told her I'd be doing a sequel.

And finally a special thanks to the new *News at Noon* team of producer Stephen Grant and story editor Jackie Kavanagh. You've all been a great help.

INTRODUCTION

In the fall of 1989, I was forty-seven years old. I don't know whether I was having a delayed midlife crisis or not, but, after working in news from the age of eighteen, I needed a change. Where could a middle-aged television news cameraman go? I decided to talk things over with my brother-in-law Wayne Brennan and he suggested that I visit his office and take a couple of tests to see if I was suited for sales. Under the clock I more or less completed the two papers. I was not surprised by the results that came back a few days later. The appraiser summed it up with this comment: "Recommend that you don't hire this person. Not suited for your type of sales operation. He or she may possibly find employment in a department store under supervision." Believe it or not, I was relieved but, in my heart of hearts, with the right product line, I know that I'd be a good salesman.

The very next day I paid a visit to Jeff Keene who was the producer of Global News at that time. "Jeff," I said, "I've been Bill Bramah's main cameraman and field producer for ten years now. Would it be possible for me to start doing some of my own human interest stories? I want to find them, shoot them, write the script, and put my own narration on them." Jeff, a man who understood, said, "Give it a try." That's all I needed to hear. For the next two years, I worked on my own stories as well as shooting the Bramah's Ontario segments. As I complete my first book, I'm into my sixth year of travelling this wonderful province as a one-man-band. I've never been happier in my career. I'm doing what I love to do best . . . positive lifestyle stories. People are actually happy to see me and it's not uncommon that I'm invited to stay for lunch.

My youngest daughter decided to get into television news as well. Dana Culbert joined CFPL Television in London, Ontario, in the fall of 1993 as a tape editor. She's also out in the field learning how to use the camera like her father. I'm really proud that she decided to get into television and it's marvellous that she's working with some of my dear friends at CFPL-TV, the station with which I began my career with in 1961. Two of my oldest friends, John Macdonald and George Clark, were both reporters when I was there, and now, as management, they've both been extremely supportive to Dana.

VANNA, HANNA, ALANA AND NORTON

QUADRUPLET CALVES

Seven-year-old Sillsway Madador Val is a registered pure-bred Holstein. If she wasn't, she should have been given the ribbon for the 1991 Mother of the Year in Durham County. She gave birth to quadruplets, three females and a baby bull. Val's had three pregnancies before, but bore only a single calf each time. The births took place on the Gordhill Farm near Cannington. Don Gordon was making his rounds of the property when he discovered Val in the back pasture; she'd given birth to triplets. He raced back to the house to get the truck and his father Ted. When they returned to the field, Val had given birth to a fourth; this one turned out to be a male. The calves weighed approximately thirty-five pounds each, about half the birth-weight of a normal calf. The main thing was they were alive and seemed well. It was a miracle birth; time would be the important factor now. The veterinarian from neighbouring Sunderland claimed it would take about three months to get through the danger period. Along with their mother's milk and loads of vitamins, Don and Ted Gordon and their hired man John Firth would give them a lot of tender loving care. Mother Val was artificially inseminated, but fertility drugs were not used. The proud sire is Hanover Hill Lieutenant, from the United Breeders in Guelph. The Gordon Family named the heifers Vanna, Hanna, and Alana. The baby bull is Norton.

The calves were born in June and I returned three months later to see how they were coming along. The weather had turned cold that morning and the wind was driving the rain hard against the barn. I set up my equipment in the paddock area and, when the door opened, I couldn't believe my eyes. Out of the barn sprang four of the friskiest calves I'd ever seen. They pulled, hopped, and bounded all around the yard with the three farmers in tow. They'd almost caught up to what would be considered normal size and weight for three-month old calves. Veterinarian Rick Doner had nothing but good things to say about the calves. "They were good strong calves at birth and they've done well," said Dr. Doner. "The odds were quite high, as a matter of fact, astronomical, that the Gordon's four calves would be alive at birth, and would do so well for so long."

When I'd finished shooting, Don invited us all in for a cup of coffee. Hollie, Don's four-year-old daughter, was proudly showing her granddad Ted a ribbon she'd won at the Sunderland Fall Fair. As a pre-4 H'er, she'd shown Vanna the week before and the little calf had placed third in its category. Sipping my coffee, I spotted a painting on the kitchen wall, a wonderful watercolour of dairy cattle grazing in a field. The artist turned out to be Don's cousin Jean Abernathy, an Ontario College of Art graduate who is an animal painter living with her family in Trenton. Well, one thing always leads to another and this would become another of my stories.

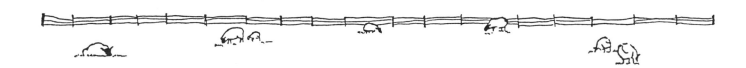

Photograph: David Cameron

Dr. John Walton and me at his farm near Rockwood. The little critter with
us came to Canada as a frozen embryo from the United Kingdom.

CHAROLLAIS LAMBS

If you were to ask me what my favourite animal is, I'd have to say the newborn lamb. To witness this beautiful little creature stagger to its feet moments after its birth is a miracle. The North Yorkshire Dales, where sheep graze by the thousands, is my favourite area in England. The television series *All Creatures Great and Small,* and the books written by the famous Yorkshire veterinarian James Herriot, helped to make me feel this way. Another reason for loving the lamb is that my wife Donna and I have lap dogs, and two of them are Bichon Frise. One of the Bichons, our Kate, not only looks like a lamb, but her coat feels like one as well.

In February of 1994, twelve Arcott ewes in the Guelph area were implanted with forty frozen embryos shipped over from the United Kingdom, and in March, ten female and eleven male lambs were born to those surrogate mothers. This was North America's debut of one of the world's most desirable sheep, the Charollais. The twenty-one lambs were born on Dr. John Walton's farm near Rockwood, Ontario. Dr.Walton is a professor of animal and poultry science at the University of Guelph. "Two things are important to the sheep industry in Ontario," said Dr. Walton, "the number of lambs you can sell and the quality of lambs you can sell. We have lots of sheep in Ontario that give you lots of lambs, but we felt that there was a need to improve the quality."

In the spring of that year I visited Dr. Walton's farm, taking Ryerson journalism student David Cameron along with me.

To protect the young lambs from outside diseases, David and I were asked to put on plastic booties. Were we a fashion statement for sure! I positioning myself in one corner of a grassy paddock, my camera mounted atop the tripod, as Dr. Walton opened the gate. It was like a scene from the wild west as the flock charged into our field. It made a marvellous scene for the story. Dr. Walton is not only the shepherd, he's a partner in Ovine Reproductive Technologies. This company is a collaborative effort with representatives from the University of Guelph, the Ontario Ministry of Agriculture and Food, the United Breeders of Guelph, and Agriculture Canada. They're part of a long-term strategy to develop artifical insemination for Ontario's sheep producers. Because federal laws in Canada require long periods of quarantine following the import of live sheep, the Charollais were imported as frozen embryos. Holding a young ram, Dr. Walton said, "I think the important thing to notice is how broad they are in the back. I think you'll see that there's a lot of meat on this animal. They're not very tall; they tend to grow sideways, not upwards. They're a really nice sheep and should cross well with other breeds, giving nice lambs. We're not in the business of making lots of money, and, if the whole project is unsuccessful, then if nothing else, we'll have brought a different set of genetics in the sheep industry to this country." The group is working to have their breed registered with the Canadian Sheep Breeders Association. Once their rams are mature, the semen will be available to interested breeders.

INTERNATIONAL HOOF TRIMMING SCHOOL

When your feet ache and your toenails are too long, you feel uncomfortable and a little out of sorts. So do dogs, cats, and the larger animals like the horse and the cow. Tom Kent of Delaware knows the problem better than most and, with this knowledge and concern for the animals' well-being, he opened the International Hoof Trimming School.

Three times a year, the John M. Walker Farms in Aylmer provide Tom with barn space and a herd of registered Holstein dairy cattle on which to demonstrate. For a fee of twenty-five hundred dollars, people from all over North America come to learn the proper way to trim hoofs. It's definitely a hands-on course. The fee covers the students' accommodation and provides them with a set of quality tools. Over a ten-day period, they are instructed by veterinarians and livestock experts in fitting cattle for the show ring.

As the founding director, Tom personally inspects and advises on every hoof that's trimmed. "Farmers always question the importance of trimming feet," says Tom. "They're not so concerned with what the hoof looks like because the hoof is usually in deep bedding. What they should be concerned with is the way the legs stand on their cow. A cow can toe-out or toe-in or her feet can be too far up underneath her. They can also be too far behind her and all this can be corrected with proper trimming."

The day I was there, it was an all-male class. The students were all from south of the border, from Pennsylvania, Maine, Michigan, and Ohio. I'd say the average age of these men would be mid-thirties. They were farmers themselves, or working people who decided to make a career change. As a qualified hoof trimmer, they'll make three to five hundred dollars a day looking after dairy herds for farmers who view this as part of a preventative maintenance program.

"If a cow gets a little bit sore, the first thing she does is lay down," said Tom. "She's off her feed, off the milk production, and the farmer begins to loose money."

Tom trims at least seven thousand cows a year himself. He claims that it takes precision, a sure hand, and a strong back. Regular hoof trimming can extend the life of the average cow and should be done at least once a year.

By the smiles on the faces of Betsy, Bertha, and Suzy Mae, they were feeling much better as they strolled out of the pedicure salon.

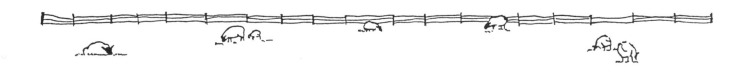

At the 1994 Royal Agricultural Winter Fair, Catherine Agar showed her Holstein heifer "Ruffles." She went on to be named the Reserve Intermediate Showperson in the Scotiabank-Hays Classic for Canadian 4-H-ers.

TEENAGE DAIRY FARMER

With so many young people leaving the farm for jobs in the city, it was a breath of fresh air to find someone who actually wanted to stay home. In the summer of 1992, I came across a young lady of sixteen, determined to remain a farmer. The morning I met Catherine Agar, she came walking into the barn wearing designer jeans and a pair of highly polished western boots. Well now, being old enough to be her dad means that I can get away with saying certain things. "Catherine," I said, "no one's going to believe you work with the cows and shovel manure if you're dressed like that." I could see she was disappointed, but she graciously went back to the farmhouse and changed. I've always been a stickler for authenticity and I know that, if I hadn't been there with my television camera, Catherine wouldn't have been so dressy. A few minutes later, she returned, still pretty as a picture, but now, with a bit of cow dung on her work boots, she looked like a real farmer.

Catherine's family call their farm "Aview Farm." It's situated in Elgin County just west of St. Thomas. The cash crop and dairy farm is run as a partnership by Catherine's father Peter, her uncle John, and her semi-retired grandfather Gordon Agar. At eighty-four, this guy was unbelievable; he looked and acted like a man at least twenty years younger. Catherine has been an intregal part of the family business since she was a little girl and has been buying and selling cattle for years. She purchased her first calf from her father at age four for sixty dollars; since then, she's built up a herd of fifteen registered Holsteins. Catherine says that women are getting into farming more than ever before. She feels that a good education is the key to becoming a successful farmer today. "I hope to go to the University of Guelph and take animal science, or something along that line," she said. "When I've completed my four years at the university, I'd like to come home and take over the farm . . . the family business."

Catherine told me that there's no way she'll ever live in the city, not even when she marries. Working with cattle is a big part of her job, but on the farm it's not uncommon to see her flinging bales of hay during harvest time. I was most impressed with this young woman. If Catherine represents the next generation of farmers, then agriculture in Canada is in good hands.

I phoned Catherine just before I finished this book and asked for a picture of her to accompany the story. She wrote back a few days later telling me that quite a few things had changed around the farm since I'd been there two and a half years ago. She went on to tell me that in February of '93, her Uncle John decided that he no longer wanted to farm; this meant that the family partnership would break up, and, by March, the cows and milk quota were sold. "With everything happening so quickly, it was hard for my dad, my grandfather, and I to decide what to do." Understandably, Catherine told me that she was upset. She decided not to sell her cattle.

She'd put an awful lot of time and money into her herd and she wasn't prepared to let them go. Her uncle John's barn now sits empty; they've taken her dad's old barn that hadn't had a cow milked in it since the late sixties, and cleaned it up.

Catherine is continuing to show her cattle with much success.

Her University of Guelph application has been sent in and by the fall of '95 she'll be enrolled as an "Aggie" in Animal Science.

Her greatest apprehension about leaving home is the fact that she'll constantly worry about her cows. Hopefully, after four years at university, she'll be able to come home and start milking her own herd. Catherine told me that to start virtually from scratch is extremely costly but, with the support of her family, she knows that things will turn out the right way. Catherine, I know it will too.

NORTHUMBERLAND COUNTY APPLES

How many times have you been driving along the eastern portion of Highway 401 and spotted the big, bright red apple sitting in the field near the village of Colborne? Well, I've driven by it dozens of times and finally I just had to check out what is billed as the world's biggest apple. Called "The Big Apple," it's now the centrepiece of a burgeoning theme park. When you enter the door at the base of the apple itself, you find the interior filled with interesting trivia like, "China is the largest producer of apples in the world." After you've climbed to the top, seen the displays, and gone out on the observation deck, you can visit the gift shop and restaurant next door. The aroma of freshly baked apple pies wafting through the air is bound to make you sit and have a slice.

Northumberland County is the fourth-largest apple producing area in Ontario. One hundred and fifteen commercial growers have devoted three thousand acres to apple trees. When I visited the orchard of Peter Wyminga, his crew was harvesting Courtlands from semi-dwarf trees. This variety is low in sugar and ascorbic acid and has become very popular with diabetics. Dave Rutherford's orchard is on the eastern outskirts of Colborne. His grandfather planted McIntosh apple trees more than seventy-five years ago. Although the McIntosh is still the most popular, Dave grows other varieties for both the commercial market and for the roadside store that his wife Pat operates. Pat began her roadside business selling apples to passing motorists from a picnic table.

"An apple that's coming on strong these days is the Empire." said Dave. "They're a cross between the Mac and the Delicious. There's quite a few of them being planted. They're a relatively new apple, maybe ten to fifteen years old. In my own opinion, the Empire will one day overtake the McIntosh in popularity." On the west side of Colborne is the Knights Big 'A' Brand Fruit Farms. The Knights Family grow and pack for worldwide consumption. They employ forty local workers for ten months each year. In 1991 they shipped 125,000 boxes of McIntosh, Empire, and Red Delicious to the United Kingdom. The family-run business began over fifty years ago.

Both the Northumberland communities of Colborne and Brighton capitalize on the number of apple orchards in their area. The village of Colborne hangs large cutouts of rosy, red apples from its main street lamp posts. The community newspaper, the *Colborne Chronicle,* adorns its masthead with a drawing of an apple. Next time you buy a bag of apples at the supermarket, check to see if they were grown in Northumberland County. There's a good chance they were.

Northumberland County apple grower Dave Rutherford turns out to be related to a colleague of mine at Global. He's a cousin of Sportsline producer Dave Rutherford and Dave's brother Paul, a reporter with *Peterborough This Week.*

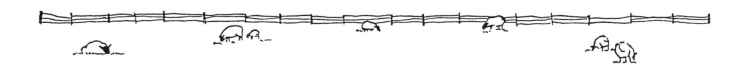

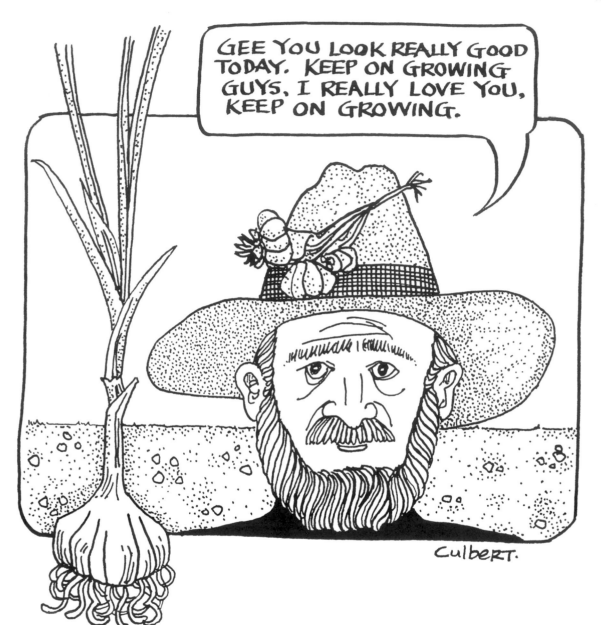

THE GARLIC MAN OF FISH LAKE

If you've been the Royal Agricultural Winter Fair in Toronto in the last few years, you may have come across Ted Maczka. He's the guy walking around with bulbs of garlic on his cowboy hat. Ted's known as the "Garlic Man of Fish Lake." He sets up a small booth and promotes garlic as a natural preventative and healing medicine.

Ted lives on a hundred-acre farm nestled on the shore of Fish Lake in Prince Edward County. His one-man operation is dedicated to making Canada self-sufficient in garlic. Leaning on his hoe, he told me: "Years ago I read that Canada imports five million dollars worth of garlic every year, so I started working on it as a backyard operation. Now I want to educate people. We can grow garlic, a much better quality than in California or anywhere else in the world, because we have the ideal climate. We have cold weather in the spring, and longer days, which helps it to grow."

"I do all my own research," he said. "I record details on every plant. Some people think I'm crazy because I talk to my plants every day." He wandered down a row of garlic plants, giving them a pep talk. "Gee, you look really good today. Keep on growing guys, I really love you. You really look good guys, keep on growing."

Ted's built himself a proper greenhouse on his property. From an elephant garlic plant, he's grown a one-pounder. He grows fifteen different varieties of garlic; they vary in bulb size and the number of cloves per bulb. The seed is planted in mid-October and harvested in mid-July the following year. Most people are not aware that the stem of the maturing plant is edible; while the bulbs are growing beneath the soil, you can snip and eat the stems. Ted also showed me how you can have fresh garlic in your home throughout the winter. He chops up the stems finely, pours olive oil over them, and then twists on an air-tight lid before placing it in the freezer. When you're making dinner on a cold, blustery winter's day, you'll have garlic that tastes much fresher than the cloves you purchase at the supermarket. It's the perfect ingredient to use when you're preparing an appetizer like bruschetta.

Ted has a number of regular customers and they agree that the quality and taste of store-bought garlic don't hold a candle to his. One of his favourite customers showed up the morning I was there. Domenic Iozzo owns the Italian Garden Restaurant in Picton, just a few miles from the farm. Seventy-five percent of the dishes that Domenic prepares have fresh garlic in them. I took a few scenes of the two of them checking out the garden, and then we paused for a cold beer. Domenic invited us over to his pickup where he magically transformed the tailgate into a picnic table. Out of a cooler came cheese, salami, and crusty Italian bread. Ted went into the house, returning with a bottle of vodka containing garlic stems; being a garlic lover myself, I found it didn't taste bad at all. Before I left Prince Edward County, I followed Domenic into Picton, where he chopped up enough stems to fill two large jars. Then he poured in the olive oil. Ted wanted me to take the garlic stems home to my wife and Domenic graciously offered to prepare it for me. This was a most enjoyable outing and another reason why I love my job. By the way, the Garlic Man of Fish Lake truly believes that garlic is a preventative medicine. Good for the ticker. But what about bad breath? Ted claims all you have to do is chew on a stalk of celery or parsley leaves and that will take the odour away.

The Colville family on their Manitoulin Island yarn farm.
Surrounding mom and dad (Deb and Bill) are, left to right,
James holding Templeton, Alex, Kathleen, and Brian cuddling
Winston.

WOOLLY HARVEST YARN FARM

I'm forever gathering story ideas from various newspapers and this one came from the *Toronto Star*. Dated the 14th of November, 1992, Frank Jones' column read: Spinning a fresh, natural lifestyle. Home for the Colvilles is a remote hundred-acre farm at the western end of Manitoulin Island. Frank wrote his story about Bill and Deb Colville while they were attending the Creative Sewing and Needlework Festival in Toronto that year. I snipped out the article and filed it away in my northern Ontario docket. One day I'd get one or two more stories up that way, making the long trip worthwhile. Two years later, I pulled it back out of the file drawer.

It was August of '94, and I had just completed my journey across Georgian Bay on the *Chi-Cheemaun*. After it docked in South Baymouth on Manitoulin Island, I headed for Evansville. After checking into my accommodation, I decided to pay the Colvilles a visit. They weren't expecting me until the next morning, but I was curious to see their operation. When I arrived, the gate at the road was shut and I figured that they must be away shopping in nearby Gore Bay. From the edge of the road I shot a few scenes of their guard donkey as it tending the flock of sheep. As the sun began to set on the largest freshwater island in the world, all was at peace. All was quiet, except . . . out behind the barn, I could hear the sound of a tractor approaching. Within moments, it came into view pulling a wagon loaded high with hay. When the family noticed me down on the road, one of the children came running and waving towards me. The gate was opened and I drove into the farmyard. It seemed that the entire family was involved in bringing in the hay. After introductions all around, Deb told me that the hay will be used as feed for the animals over the long, cold winter. The Colvilles lifted the rectangular bales from the wagon onto a conveyor belt to be stored in the barn.

James, Alex, Kathleen, and Brian were a tremendous help to their parents. I shot scenes of them working silhouetted against the setting sun. After the hay was off-loaded, the family climbed aboard again to return to the fields. As they headed towards the back forty, they all waved goodbye. They'd carry on working that evening until the sun sank below the horizon; then they'd do it all again tomorrow.

Deb and Bill are originally from Downsview, part of Metropolitan Toronto. They met in high school and attended the University of Guelph together. She studied plant pathology and he microbiology.

So, I asked them, why a sheep farm?

"We met a lot of interesting students at Guelph, many of them right off the farm," said Deb. "Before we bought our own place, we spent a lot of time working in the labs of the university.. In my particular lab there were no windows; you couldn't get any fresh air if you wanted. So, after two years of that, I decided I needed a bit of fresh air and that's why we decided to change our plans a bit." And change they did, the first thing being their priorities.

Deb now tends animals instead of plants, and Bill grows vegetables. "The important thing to me about the sheep is the manure that they produce," says Bill, "because that's what I use to put on my garden. I have about an acre of garden and I take my produce to two farmers' markets, one in Gore Bay and the other in Providence Bay. I've also been providing a couple of restaurants with fresh vegatables and fruit."

At least once a year, Bill trucks their raw wool to the east coast, to MacAusland's Woollen Mills in Bloomfield, Prince Edward Island. There the wool is washed and spun to perfection. Bill returns to Manitoulin Island with clean skeins of wool which he dyes into dozens of wonderful colours. Then he hangs them on extension ladders in the yard to dry. When they're completely dry, he spins the skeins on a ballwinder into individual balls and a band of paper with the farm logo, "Woolly Harvest Manitoulin Yarns," is slipped over every ball. The front porch of their farmhouse has become a store. When I visited the farm, the Woolly Yarn flock consisted of twenty ewes, forty lambs, and three Angora goats. "It's a wonderful life," Deb told me.

Just a footnote about Frank Jones, the columnist who wrote this original story. In June of 1984, British Airways and the British Tourist Board sponsored a media race from Toronto, County Durham in England to Toronto, Ontario. The event was held to help celebrate the bicentennial of the Ontario city. Frank Jones represented the *Toronto Star* and

I was part of a fun-loving trio made up of two of my close friends. Joe Coté, then host of CBC Radio's *Metro Morning,* now host of *Ontario Morning,* and Paul Dalby, Global Television News reporter. Joe went as Lord Simcoe, a role that he'd played for the City of Toronto on Simcoe Day for many years. Paul and I went as Lord Simcoe's escorts. We were dressed in monks' habits that Joe had borrowed from the CBC wardrobe department.

This trip will always be a highlight in my life and I'm sure for everyone else that took part. The winners were columnist Mark Bonokowski and photo journalist Ken Kerr of the *Toronto Sun*. Mark is now the editor of the *Ottawa Sun.* Had Joe, Paul and I known that the prize was a return round-trip ticket to the U.K., we'd not have had so much fun stopping at so many pubs and fish and chip shoppes along the way.

LONDON, ENGLAND • JUNE 25, 1984.

Photograph: Sidney Harris, Ltd., London

Media Fun Race of 1984, sponsored by British Airways and the British Tourist Authority. Enroute to Canada, we attended a cocktail party at Ontario House in London. *Toronto Star* reporter Frank Jones is standing third from right wearing a top hat. Next to Frank is Lyn Munro. She was the bicentennial co-ordinator, Office of the Agent General for Ontario, U.K. CBC Radio's Joe Coté is fifth from right, and Paul Dalby and I are the pair of monks on the running board.

Photograph: Rick Sterritt

December 1994. Spencer and Hepburn are two happy dogs these days, thanks to Jan Sterritt (centre) who saved their lives. The beagles' adopted parents are Kevin Johnstone and Jennifer McTavish.

ABANDONED BEAGLES

I was packing up to go home from work when the phone on my desk rang. It was a farmer from the Brampton area with a plea for help. Jan Sterritt had temporarily adopted two abandoned beagles. Some heartless person had tossed the two animals out in the freezing cold on the 13th of December. They had walked up the laneway of the Sterritt's Cedarsands Beef Farm. Jan's husband Rick happened to be outside at the time and called her. Noticing that the dogs didn't have collars or identification tags, she drove them to the Brampton Animal Shelter where she was told that, if the owners weren't found or if the dogs weren't adopted within ten days, they'd be put down. Shelter foreman Jesse Reed blamed the long recession on this ever-increasing problem. "People are falling on hard times," he said. "They can't afford the animals, so they take them out to the country sideroads and dump them off, forcing the animals to fend for themselves. A lot of the time they end up in the shelter's lap."

During those desperate ten days, Jan did everything humanly possible to find the owners as there was absolutely no way that this animal lover would see the beagles put down. She placed ads in four newspapers and sent out flyers describing the cuddly, good-natured male and female. There was no response, so she brought the orphans home to the farm. Because she already had a cat and two dogs living in the house, the beagles were given a cozy bed in the milk-parlour of the barn and named Cookie and Crumbs. On camera she said, "The point I want to get across to the public is not to abandon their animals. In this type of weather, it's not fair to them they can freeze so easily. There are many no-kill shelters that pets can be taken to. Just because there's a barn in the background doesn't necessarily mean they're going to be cared for. It's not fair to the animals. They're the silent, innocent victims here, and they need to be taken care of."

These little critters were lucky to to have stumbled upon someone like Jan during one of the coldest winters on record. I came on camera with a plea on behalf of Jan and the dogs. "Cookie and Crumbs are two wonderful, older beagles that deserve a special loving home," I said, "and Jan's only willing to give them up if someone adopts them together."

Not all stories have a happy ending, but this one does. On the 14th of February, 1994, I received a letter from Jan which read:

"Dear Terry: Well, the last page of our story is finally complete. Cookie and Crumbs have been successfully adopted by a young couple in Toronto. Thanks for your help, Jan."

The young couple were Jennifer McTavish and Kevin Johnstone. On a warm and sunny Saturday morning in March, I went to their home to do a follow-up story. The canines looked well and happy with their new parents. It was obvious they were loved. One change had been made though: Cookie and Crumbs had been renamed Spencer and Hepburn.

Sitting on the back porch, Kevin said, "We were out to a restaurant for dinner on Valentine's Day and we were amazed that all we were talking about were the dogs. Jennifer asked me what we talked about before we had them. We've started to feel like real parents to them."

"If someone had told me that I'd be setting my alarm for three in the morning to let the dogs out for a pee," said Jennifer, "I would never have believed them."

Jan still gets to see the dogs because she and her husband Rick have become friends with Jennifer and Kevin. To Jan Sterritt, the farmer who saved the beagles from certain death and to Jennifer and Kevin who adopted them: I think you're terrific people.

THE DONKEY
SANCTUARY
OF CANADA

Logo courtesy of The Donkey Sanctuary of Canada.

DONKEY SANCTUARY

My friend Jan Sterritt, a Brampton-area farmer, wrote me a letter in April of '94, telling me about the Donkey Sanctuary of Canada. Jan is an animal lover of the highest order and a volunteer friend of the Sanctuary. I met her earlier that year when she had saved the lives of two dogs that had been abandoned during one of the coldest winters on record. Jan thought perhaps I could do a story about the wonderful and caring people that offered a safe haven for unwanted donkeys, hinnies, and mules. I phoned Jan after receiving the letter and told her that I'd love to do it.

Just to the south of Guelph is the Donkey Sanctuary of Canada. One hundred-acres of rolling land is a safe place of refuge for neglected, unwanted, and abused animals. Sandra Pady and her dedicated staff believe that all creatures on earth have the right to live according to their genetic, biological, and psychological needs. Out on the pasture, Sandra described what had happened to one of them. "Julie was thrown into the back of a truck with some wild horses from Arizona. She was tossed in as an afterthought. Julie lived under the most appalling conditions for the first five or six years of her life."

Then she showed me Monty, a miniature donkey. He had been purchased by a family as a pet and, as so often happens, they tired of him. Monty was put into a stall and fed, but, for the next six months he wasn't exercised, nor was his stall cleaned out. Then, fortunately for little Monty, the Humane Society stepped in.

Twenty-year-old Clint came to the farm during Christmas dinner of '93. He was undernourished and dehydrated and his hoofs were in such bad shape that it will take at least six more months for him to walk properly again. As he lay on clean straw in the nursery corral in front of Sandra's house, he was being given herbal aspirin several times a day.

Sandra, a former high school teacher with a masters in anthropology, has had a lifelong interest in animals. "As one person I do not want to be hit, starved or tied and held in one place hour after hour after hour. And we consider that the animals aren't suited to that either." When she and her husband first bought the farm, they purchased a few sheep. When she learned of a special group of conservationists called "The Rare Breeds Conservancy," she offered to care for three of their donkeys. The Conservancy, located in Marmora, Ontario, is trying to preserve our agricultural heritage. Then, one day, Sandra was alerted that ten donkeys were going to be shipped to a slaughterhouse. She put a stop to that and those animals are now living a wonderful life at the Sanctuary. A well-cared-for and healthy donkey can live to the ripe old age of forty-five.

The Donkey Sanctuary of Canada is the only one of its kind in North America. They welcome school children, seniors' clubs, and other organizations to visit the farm and be with the animals. Volunteer Friends of the Sanctuary are available to give lectures at the farm and beyond. They've also started an annual Donkey Day, where visitors are able to take nature walks and learn first-hand about these genteel equines. They can even take a ride in a replica of a nineteenth-century doctor's cart pulled by a donkey. The federal government has granted the non-profit corporation a license as a charity. One of their major concerns is the vastness of our country as the Sanctuary wants to be able to accept all donkeys that need a home, regardless of where they are in Canada. To do this they need volunteers that own a horse trailer and are willing to help transport for a distance of at least one hundred kilometres. They have been asked many times about breeding and their reply is always the same . . . "We don't breed, we don't sell, and we don't buy animals. But we do promise to give them the best home possible for the rest of their lives."

This Cotswold ewe seems quite content in the company of Jy Chiperzak
and his Australian Shepherds, Jazz and Tango.

THE RARE BREEDS CONSERVANCY

Over the past few years there's been a decline in many older breeds of cattle, sheep, poultry, and swine throughout the world. Some of these animals, are on the verge of extinction. This is primarily due to selective breeding for high industrial productivity. I was fortunate to hear about a group of conservationists that is trying to preserve some of these breeds. The group calls itself the Rare Breeds Conservancy and they're located on Joywind Farm near Marmora in eastern Ontario. Jy Chiperzak, a former documentary filmmaker, who used to raise sheep part-time, runs the farm and was the founder of the group. It's composed of dedicated volunteers who are trying to keep at least four dozen breeds of farm animals from dying out. Their success rate with the Irish Kerry cattle, for example, has been fairly good. "When we started with the breed in 1987," said Jy, "there were only ten cows and two bulls in North America. We now have about fifty animals in our network of breeders, and this has become a major proportion of the existing animals in the world." With limited space at Joywind Farm, Jy has animals placed with thirty other farmers across Canada. He showed me a Karakul Fat-Tailed Sheep. "This is a young ram," he said. "They're noted for producing pelts for Persian lamb coat production. But for us, their fat tails are an important genetic trait.

They store all their body fat in their tail as an emergency reserve for very droughty times. With the changing climatic conditions in the future, we may very well need such an important trait."

Rare-breeds conservation can be looked at as a preservation of our agricultural heritage as well. Many of these breeds are a direct link to the stock that was brought over from Europe during the colonization of North America. Jy took me to the pasture where I shot scenes of a rare Przewalski horse guarding a flock of sheep and a handful of goats. When the horse sensed danger in the air, he lowered his head against one of the sheep and gently nudged it along. By doing this a couple of times, he soon had the whole flock on the move to safer ground. It was a wonderful sight to see. The Przewalski is the last breed of wild horse in North America and, other than the one at Joywind Farm, they can only be found in zoos.

The biggest problem for the Conservancy is funding; they require money for their day-to-day operation and for the continued growth and expansion of their projects. "Twenty, fifty, or a hundred years from now, our world will be a very different place," said Jy. "We'll need the broad genetic diversity that resides in these breeds."

My wife Donna with Ernie, our tough thirteen pound
Yorkshire Terrier.

HEARTWORM IN DOGS

Dogs have been part of my family since I was a boy. Laddy was our family dog in Lucan. While we were living in the Beach area of Toronto when my daughters Sarah and Dana were young, a stray walked into our lives. She was a beauty, not beautiful, but darn handsome, and we kept her and named her Annie. For almost a decade now, my wife Donna and I have had four dogs: Ernie, a giant thirteen-pound Yorkshire Terrier; and Sean, a Lhasapoo who looked much like a bear cub before Donna gave him a haircut. Then there' our darling ladies, Kate and Holly; they're Bichon Frise. Sean unfortunately developed an incurable illness and had to be put down. For the past three years of his life, he became more and more aggressive, to the point where he couldn't be trusted with our other dogs or little children. I don't think I've ever felt as sad as I did that morning. As I held him, my little buddy died in my arms. To this day I wonder if I did the right thing.

Dogs and cats, like no other living creatures, become so much a part of the family. All they want is love and a full belly. They're always there for you. There are days when you arrive home from work feeling a little out of sorts and how do they greet you? The same way that they did yesterday and the day before, with their tails wagging ninety miles an hour, because they're happy to see you. Ernie has that Yorkshire Terrier trait; he actually shows his teeth and smiles. So, when you hear about a disease like heartworm, a disease that kills our precious little creatures, you'll do anything to protect them from it.

Heartworm is spread by the common mosquito. Once confined to the southern United States, harboured in the state of Florida and around the Mississippi River's coastal area, it has moved steadily northward over the past few years. Today it has become a serious threat to canines in southern Ontario and cottage country as well. Heartworm disease is caused by a worm that lives in the dog's heart and adjoining blood vessels. It is the most serious condition that can befall your dog and it's almost impossible to prevent your dog from being bitten by mosquitos. Heartworm will attack any canine, no matter the size, the breed, or the length of its hair.

I did my story on heartworm a few years ago. Our neighbourhood has an abundance of dogs, so it was easy to illustrate what healthy pooches look like. Along with making stars of our four, I included the Fedorak's Golden Retriever Maggie and the Bullock's beautiful Retriever pup, Skye.

Unionville's Bridle Trail Veterinary Clinic is right at the end of our street. We're fortunate that we can walk our gang down to visit the two great vets, Dr. Jim Lott and Dr. Wayne Harding. Dr. Lott and his right-hand lady Julie Smith showed what a pet owner would see on a routine heartworm visit. Your veterinarian takes a small blood sample for analysis. It's quite painless and the results are available in a day or so. If the test comes back negative, which almost every one does, the preventative program begins. Over the years, researchers and chemists have developed the medication from a one-a-day pill to what we're using now, a once-a-month chewable candy. Our gang loves it. As dog owners become aware of this disease and put their pets on the preventative program, the less the disease will spread. The average life span of a dog is fourteen years; we owe it to them and our families to make sure they live full and healthy lives.

Culbert.

HAIRLESS FELINES

I love all animals and we have three small dogs of our own, but there are two animals that I dearly love but can't have because of allergies, the horse and the cat. One day I read an article in the newspaper about hairless felines. Linda Birks, the breeder, claimed that they are the perfect pet for people who suffer from allergies. Linda is the only breeder of hairless cats in Canada and operates Aztec Sphynx Cattery from her home in Sarnia. I set up an appointment with her to do the story.

When I first laid eyes on the little critters, they reminded me of one of the little characters from the movie *Star Wars.* Their skin is suede-like and wrinkled from head to toe. Their ears seem overly large. Their eyes are large also, lemon-shaped and slant toward the outer edge of their ears. Linda told me that I would need to go beyond their curious looks to see their intelligence, personality, and loyalty. She claims that cuddling these animals is almost like handling a baby. The unusual appearance of the hairless cat has drawn some derogatory remarks. "What kind of dog is that?" "It looks like a rat." "Why did you shave it?" "What constitutes a cat is something that's very cuddly, soft and furry, in most people's minds," said Linda. "What I'm trying basically to do with this breed is to educate people.

Just because they happen to be hairless does not mean that they are less devoted or loving. They can be a cherished pet that any member of the family can learn to love and appreciate."

The hairless Sphynx is the world's rarest breed. There are just over five hundred worldwide, eight of which live with Linda. Bambi, her fifteen-year old, is the oldest hairless Sphynx in the world. This class of cat is the result of a rare but natural genetic mutation within domestic litters. It literally dates back to the pharaohs of Egypt; evidence shows that companionship between man and the cat began in Egyptian households as far back as 2000 B.C.

Linda claims that the indoor tabbies don't require special attention other than a bath every second day to remove a buildup of sweat and oil. The starting price is two thousand dollars Canadian for a Sphynx. Linda has never had or heard of a bad-tempered Sphynx. "They're lively, inquisitive and full of mischief," she told me. From my personal observations, I'd have to agree. The truly amazing thing for me was being in the same room with these cats for about two and a half hours and not having the slightest hint of a wheeze. This was proof to me that someone with allergies could have a pet.

Pen and ink by John Doherty

The earliest moon of wintertime is not so round and fair as was the
ring of glory on the helpless infant there.

FOLKLORE and LEGENDS

As a young lad growing up in England, John Doherty had a fascination with the folklore and legend of the North American Indian. As an artist, that fascination has remained with him to this day. In his early teens he started collecting antique taxidermy, and a prize possession is his European Owl that dates back to 1890. John met his Canadian wife Debbie in the late 1970s while she was on an extended vacation in England. She'd taken a year off as a registered nurse to work on a farm in Somerset.

Debbie discovered John working at his father's four hundred-year-old pub, The Rock Inn. He was the cook, selling his paintings on the side. They came to Canada in 1982.

"The Indian people appeal to me greatly because their legends and mythology tie closely with nature and the environment in which they lived," said John. "The birds and the animals of this country are very important to them, both as a source of inspiration and as a source of food and clothing."

"Every picture tells a story" is the theme for his paintings. Intrigued with the tales, songs, prayers, and magic of our First Nations people, John paints in his Port Hope home/studio which he calls the Old Lodge Gallery. The versatility and skill of this artist may be seen in the variety of media he's chosen to work with. John has illustrated hundreds of kayak and ottertail paddles over the years. Not only does he illustrate the paddle, but he also incorporates the legend in printed words. "The words are very important," John told me. "The irony of this whole thing is that the words were written down by the early white reformists and missionaries. The Indians had no written language, so the dichotomy is this: we were wiping out their civilization at the same time we were recording it."

In an odd way, John Doherty reminded me of another Englishman by the name of Archibald Belaney. Archibald was born in 1888 and raised in Hastings, England. He too was fascinated with North American Indians and emigrated to Canada in 1906, seventy-six years before John. Archibald settled in the Temagami region of Northern Ontario where he lived with a band of Ojibwa. He was a conservationist. Calling himself Grey Owl, he claimed that his father was a Scot and his mother an Apache.

I went for a pub lunch with John and Debbie after we'd finished the story. As we chatted, I mentioned the other types of stories that I do, including positive agriculture. It turned out that, not long before I did the story with John, I'd done one on his brother-in-law, Mark Ritchie. Mark is a sheep farmer and a professional "have shears will travel," sheep shearer. I shot his story in the summertime at his rented farm in Prince Edward County. Since then, Mark and his family have bought a farm on Amherst Island near Kingston and are heavily into sheep breeding. Mark's wife Cherry is the sister of John Doherty's wife Debbie. Small world.

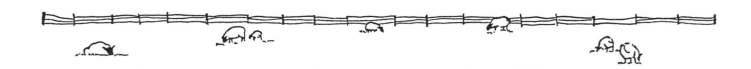

SIX-MILE-BRIDGE

Six-Mile-Bridge, County Clare, Ireland. Publican Paddy Casey and Global's Bob McAdorey holding a painting by London, Ontario artist Brian Lambert.

In the spring of '93, Bob McAdorey and I travelled to Ireland. Both the McAdorey and Culbert families emigrated to Canada from the Emerald Isle. Over a two-week period, we shot eight stories throughout the north and south and had enough material left over to make up a half-hour show which we used the following St. Patrick's Day. A portion of our time was spent in County Clare. One of our day trips took us to Craggaunowen and the Hunt Museum. Craggaunowen Castle was built by a John Mac-Sheeda around 1550. Standing a few yards from the castle was a modernistic glass pyramid and, floating inside, was a leather boat called a curragh, with square sails bearing a Celtic cross. This unique craft crossed the Atlantic Ocean in the years 1976-77. It was a full-size replica of the one used in the legendary voyage of St. Brendan the Navigator. Irish legend insists that St. Brendan reached America in a similar craft, almost a thousand years before Columbus. From the pyramid, we walked a long path to the crannog. Joined to the land by a wooden causeway, the crannog is an artificial island which provided the base for a secure homestead. It was defended by water and a stout palisade. It represented a pattern of Irish life that was established as far back as the Stone Age.

After Bob and I had finished our story at this historic tourist attraction, we headed back along the winding road towards Bunratty. We were staying at a hotel next door to the famous Bunratty Castle. Enroute, our thirst got the better of us. As we passed through the village of Six-Mile-Bridge, our rental car veered to the left, coming to a full stop at the front door of Casey's Pub. Inside, as the only customers, we each partook of a pint of Smithwicks. This brewery, established in 1710, is now owned by Guinness of Dublin. As I scanned the walls of the pub, my eyes came to rest on a painting, a good likeness of the exterior of the very building that we were in. Paddy Casey, the publican, hearing our accents, asked where we were from. When I said Canada, he went on to tell us it was a Canadian on holidays who had painted it and had given it to him as a gift. No doubt for a few pints, I thought to myself. Paddy took it from the wall and flipped it over, revealing the artist's name and a post-office box number in London, Ontario, on the reverse side. All of a sudden this became a possible story. Feeling that there was a fifty-fifty chance of finding the Canadian artist, I took some picturesque shots of the village on my television camera and a couple of scenes of Bob and Paddy Casey standing in front of the pub holding the painting. If I could find the artist, I would have myself a story with an Irish connection. On our return to Toronto, I wrote the artist in London explaining my good fortune in Ireland. I asked in the letter if he'd consider doing a story with me. As I mailed it off, I half expected to never receive a reply, but I did. Brian Lambert answered me and another 'Culbert story' was born.

Brian's home and studio is on Adelaide Street in London and, at the time of my visit, he was writing and illustrating a comic book. Titled "*Songs for the Chamelion,*" it's a story of self-discovery in the form of a psychological fantasy. In the comic book, a woman named Marcy discovers her emotional freedom through dreams, which transport her from North America to the west coast of Ireland. Brian finds that many of his inspirations come from that country, and this is reflected in many of his paintings as well. With a grandfather from Dublin and a grandmother from Clare, his roots in Ireland run deep. He returns every second year to draw and paint, quite often staying in Six-Mile-Bridge, where he frequents Casey's Pub. "One of the most important elements of my art, and my personality I guess, is that I love people," said Brian. "In Ireland I really find it quite easy to approach people and they're very often open to it. Even the most seemingly shy people are very open to casual conversation. It's so nice going into the pubs there. Even in a little village, you can sit down and immediately find someone to talk to."

Brian not only paints and draws cartoons, he's also a sculptor and a designer and maker of fine leather products. Then add to all this his music; he plays the sax and has quite a recording studio set up in his home. One of my favourite pieces was a haunting composition he did on the horn which he combined with train sounds that he'd recorded at the Limerick City railway station. I used this music in the story I did with him.

It's interesting and a lot of fun for me, finding my stories. I'd probably never have met this multi-talented artist if Bob and I hadn't stopped for a pint in Six-Mile-Bridge, County Clare, Ireland.

Suzette McDougall painting from the human figure in her Carriage
House Studio.

THE FEMALE FIGURE

When Suzette McDougall completes a painting, she often takes it to Sun Art on St. Andrew Street in Fergus. There, owner and fellow artist Tony Sepers helps her choose the proper matte and frame to complement her work. Suzette has always had a love for art and told me that over the years her supportive mother gave her approval to countless drawings and paintings that she'd done on their family farm. She was always drawing horses, birds, and other animals that lived near their home in the country. After graduating from high school, she went on to the University of Guelph. There she took a minor in Business Administration and a major in fine arts. Today she works as a secretary/ bookkeeper at her husband's parents' window and door business in neighbouring Elora. Her liberated husband Scott loves to cook, enabling Suzette to spend all her spare time drawing and painting. She works at an easel in a large area that Scott constructed for her within their Fergus home. Totally surrounded by her own finished paintings, she calls her space the Carriage House Studio.

Suzette's subject matter of late has been dominated by the clothed or nude figure. Her style of painting has been greatly influenced by Matisse and Van Gogh. "After visiting New York City and the works of Matisse," said Suzette, "I began to paint the nude figure. Since viewing his collection, I've delved into it whole-heartedly. It's been an exercise in exploring colour, composition, and form. I have been particularly interested in trying to convey the state of the human condition. I use animal and human figures alone or in a combination to convey an emotional or spiritual state. A lot of people ask me why I haven't many male models depicted in my paintings. To be quite honest, they're hard to come by. I don't know whether men are insecure about their figures or what. It's also been a tradition throughout history to use the female figure. Hopefully that will change someday."

Her figurative work can be either realistic or simplistic. Her style can be characterized as rich in colour and bold in form. Suzette generally works with a live model, either in her own studio or with a group of artists that hire one, and is often able to complete a canvas during a sitting. She also works from sketches made during model sessions, and reworks and reduces these sketches to their simplest forms at home. This process of reduction has translated well into another medium, the woodcut.

"I enjoy using a variety of mediums," says Suzette, "ranging from oils, monoprints, woodcuts, watercolour, and collage. There are times when I tire of the same old thing. I lose interest in my pursuits so, to refresh and challenge myself, I'll try something different." Not all her work is in a serious vein as she paints landscapes and other subjects filled with a light-hearted and whimsical spirit.

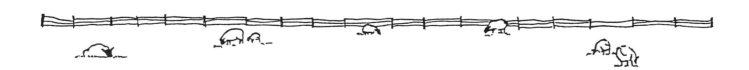

Yosemite Sam Radoff with two automobiles he customized, and "The Sam Radoff Sculptural Award for Excellence" that he designed and sculpted.

YOSEMITE SAM RADOFF

My father passed away in 1958; he was just thirty-eight years old. I was sixteen at the time. The year before he died, he'd purchased a four-door Pontiac V8. It was robin's-egg blue with a white top and a white panel running through its middle. It was a sharp-looking automobile and extremely fast. When Dad was alive, he didn't want me driving his car, so he bought me an old British-made Prefect. Somewhere along the trail my dark-blue "perfect Prefect" gave up and my mother, after Dad had gone, allowed me to use the Pontiac once in a while. The year Dad died, I quit school and went to work for a wholesale drygoods firm in London. Then I decorated the Pontiac: I installed two sexy blue lights behind the windshield and got rid of the factory-made hubcaps, replacing them with the latest rage, spun aluminum wheel discs; from the antenna I hung multi-coloured plastic ribbons. My friends and I would drive from Lucan into the big city of London and curb-cruise along Dundas Street, checking out the babes. I got away with these decorative accessories for a couple of months; then one day, one of my mother's friends queried her about it. That was it . . . game over. Every male I know has had a love affair with at least one car in his life. Most of those guys personalized their car or truck in some way or another.

Enough of my misspent youth, because the real story is about Yosemite Sam. I had the honour of visiting Sam and his wife Cheri at their home in Delaware, just west of London. His real name is Sam Radoff and he grew up during the 1940s in Detroit. As a little boy he was interested in automobiles and could always be found hanging around the local autobody shops. He had a natural talent with paints and brushes, and a mother who was full of encouragement. By the time he was thirteen, he was pinstriping cars at auto shows. At fourteen, Sam chopped, restructured, and painted a 1932 Ford Sedan for a customer behind the house in the family garage. In 1968 Sam opened his own commercial shop, specializing in custom cars and motorcycles. His brother Jim joined him as a partner, specializing in cartoons and lettering. In 1971 he was presented with the International Show Car Association's Award for Best New American Artist. On permanent display at The Museum of Modern Art in Zurich, Switzerland, is a custom, gold-plated, hand-painted motorcycle that he did for daredevil Evil Knievel.

Sam's life changed in 1982 when he met and married Cheri Oliver of Delaware. Sam gave his brother Jim his half of the business, sold his house and property, and moved to Canada. Yosemite Sam the automotive artist became Sam Radoff the fine art sculptor. With no formal training, no education in fine art or art history, Sam began to sculpt. "Most people think my scuptures are stone or marble," said Sam, "but they're actually welded steel. Each sculpture that I do is welded from ten, twenty, one hundred pieces of steel, hand formed. Then I weld them together, grind, re-weld, grind, re-weld, grind until I can get it smooth enough to finish with an acrylic base. Sculpture should be something that you can touch and feel because it's a personal thing. I don't title anything because I want people to form their own opinion and their own thoughts about what I do."

The day I did the story, a couple of Sam's friends had come over from Strathroy with their cars that he had customized. Bob Goddard drove his 1934 Ford Coupe replica and Marilyn Dejonckheere had a '57 Ford Fairlane 500. The cars and a number of Sam's sculptures illustrated his past life and his exciting new one. As I was leaving, Sam and Cheri were packing for a trip to Gettysburg, Pennsylvania. Sam had designed and made a sculpture that he was presenting as an award at a prestigious custom car show that weekend. It was 'The Sam Radoff Sculptural Award For Excellence.'

Alexander Krajewski's "Waiting For Spring" is typical of the old Ontario houses the Paris watercolourist loves to paint.

HIS LOVE OF BUILDINGS

Alexander Krajewski can't understand why Canadians tear down old buildings just to put up something new. Born in Warsaw, he spent several of his childhood years in the United States. He's travelled extensively to Indonesia, Egypt, Singapore, Germany, France, and Denmark. It was through these travels that he learned to appreciate the different cultures, landscapes, and architectures. Alexander went on to study architecture. He was taught the European style, which meant learning to draw buildings by hand, viewing them as works of art. I met Alexander and his artist wife Anna at their combination home, studio, workshop, and gallery in Paris, Ontario. I was in their town doing a story on the festival called "Springtime in Paris." The Krajewskis discovered Paris when they were travelling between their home in Toronto and London, Ontario. They were attracted by the name initally, because they had met and married in Paris, France. They eventually found the building that was just right for them. They call their studio Gallery 61, because it's at 61 Grand River Street North. If you look at the back of their building and the others that join it, you'd swear that you were in Europe. The Grand River itself passes right below their studio and living quarters. I was most impressed with this couple and their little Yorkshire terrier named Frederick. I returned a few months later to do their story.

After studying architecture, Alexander's desire for artistic expression found him working as a furniture and interior designer, and as an illustrator. Gradually, painting, which had always fascinated him, became the dominant part of his life. In 1983, he devoted himself exclusively to fine art, watercolour being his favorite medium. His admiration for the beauty of Canada's nature and its heritage is evident in his unforgettable landscape and still-life paintings. Alexander has a love for turn-of-the-century houses.

"When I select the subject for my painting," he said, "I don't just show the house standing in the middle of the field or the middle of the lawn, I walk around it to find the best angle from which to paint it."

At the time of my visit, the Krajewskis had just returned from Europe. The result of that trip was a whole new collection of original paintings which they were getting ready to show the public. Frederick had even gone with them. When I did the story, Anna had taken a break from painting and was working as her husband's full-time agent and publisher. She'd also taken charge of framing Alexander's paintings and felt she could be more objective about choosing the proper matting and frames. Today Anna is back painting in watercolour, and calls what she does country traditional still-life.

Alexander's limited edition prints are published from his original watercolour paintings, each print being carefully inspected, signed and numbered by the artist. Then the printing plate is cut up into numbered pieces and quite often the plate fragment will be included in the matte that's used in framing the print.

After a most enjoyable morning with Anna and Alexander, I was invited to stay for lunch. Over a glass of wine and a couple slices of pizza, we sat overlooking the Grand River. It really was like being in Europe, with the view from their apartment window and the wonderful accents of my hosts. It was one of those days that I thoroughly enjoyed.

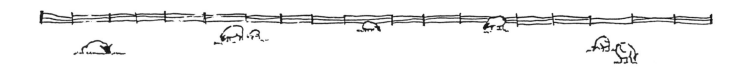

Paul Duff painting what he loves best, the Bruce Peninsula. At the age of twenty-two, Paul exhibited in a juried show with A. Y. Jackson, A. J. Casson, and Lawren Harris.

PAINTER OF THE BRUCE

I must admit that I'd never heard of Paul Duff, a painter of flowers, wildlife, woodland and marine scenes, until the day Nancy White gave me his brochure. Nancy works at Global in the on-air promotions department and knows Paul Duff because her parents are his next-door neighbours just north of Wiarton on the Bruce Peninsula. When I first made contact with Paul, I told him that he would be the first story on my trip to Manitoulin and St. Joseph Islands; I had arranged to do five features over a six-day journey that would start at his place. "Don't book yourself into a motel," said Paul, "you'll stay overnight with the wife and me." Well, needless to say, I was most impressed with his offer. This genuine show of hospitality to a stranger doesn't happen much anymore. So, without hesitation, I took him up on it.

Colpoy's Bay and the Bruce Peninsula are daily inspirations to this woodland and wildlife artist. In the early 80s, Paul and his Swiss-born wife Leila built a gorgeous two-storey log home in the bush just north of Mar. Paul was born on the 15th of January 1928, in Hamilton. He was the only undergraduate in pre-medicine to give a lecture in fine art at McMaster University. After graduating from Hamilton Teachers' College, he earned his living as an itinerant teacher in Brazil and Switzerland. In Geneva, he spent two years painting and teaching at the International School. At the age of twenty-two, Paul exhibited in a juried show with three members of the Group of Seven, A. Y. Jackson, A. J. Casson and Lawren Harris. He was officially recognized by the National Gallery of Canada as a Canadian Painter in 1956.

His paint brushes and sketch pad literally saved his hide a number of times. While travelling by ship from Brazil to New York City, Paul ran up a bar bill of five hundred dollars entertaining fellow passengers on board. When he discovered that there was no way to pay the tab, he pulled out his tools of the trade and sold portraits to anyone that wanted one painted. He actually ended up with money in his pocket by the time the ship docked. Paul settled back in Canada for nine years between 1956 and '65, then he was off to Brazil again. This time he stayed and worked until 1981. While living in Rio de Janeiro, he was invited to show at the National Gallery of Brazil. For his work as an artist and teacher during his time in that country, he was made an Honorary Citizen of Rio de Janeiro and a member of the Order of Honorary Cariocas. Paul was the first Canadian to ever receive these honours.

Paul's first wife was Brazilian and two of their three grown children still live in that country. On his return to Canada in 1981, he discovered the Bruce Peninsula. Paul's often been told that he's Canada's best-kept secret. Even the locals refer to his art gallery as the jewel of the Bruce. "The Bruce Peninsula is probably the most beautiful place in the world as far as I'm concerned," he said. "I've painted in Brazil, along the Amazon, and in Switzerland. I've been commissioned to paint castles in Scotland a number of times, but it is really wonderful to be home, and home is where the heart is, and that's the Bruce Peninsula." He often captures nature right on his own ten-acre property. He's a strong supporter of the Federation of Ontario Naturalists and the Bruce Trail Association. With his

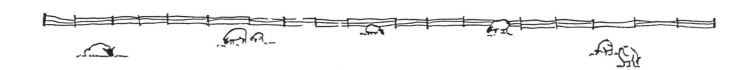

French-designed portable paint box and easel set up on its tripod legs, I shot scenes of Paul painting the tranquil and serene vista. He never uses a camera because he has a photographic memory. If he doesn't complete the painting on location, he just stores the image away in his mind, finishing it at a later date in his studio. Paul's paintings are all original; you won't find a numbered print in his gallery because he doesn't believe in commercialism. His paintings can be found in private collections throughout the world. When I asked the artist, linguist, educator, and psychologist if he had a favourite painting, he replied, "The next one that I paint."

I spent a wonderful evening with the Duffs. We finished shooting late that afternoon and then I was taken on a tour of their magnificent log home with Swiss and Scottish memorabilia displayed throughout. Leila showed me tiny miniature Swiss houses that her grandmother had made, and I could imagine Heidi and her cows on the pastureland leading up to the Alps. The little houses were beautiful. As Leila prepared dinner, Paul and I enjoyed a glass or two of his homemade beer. After the scrumptious meal was over, we sat and made old-fashioned conversation without watching television. The next morning after a hearty breakfast, I bid farewell to the Duffs and their two adorable canines. I headed north on Highway 6 for Tobermory. I had to be there before eleven to get shots of Ontario Northlands *Chi-Cheemaun* arriving from Manitoulin Island. The twentieth birthday of that ship was my next story.

Photograph: Leila Duff

After dinner conversation in the Duff's home included their dogs, Amy and Jenny.

Howdenvale Wetlands, Bruce Peninsula. This beautiful springtime painting by Paul Duff measures 24" x 36".

Songbird Carver Woody Woodward at his studio in Flesherton. Perched on his fingers are his carvings of a Western Tanager and an immature Wood Thrush.

SONGBIRD CARVER

Global cameraman Bill Barker and his wife Ann Romer, the host of *Breakfast Television* on CITY TV, have a country home on the outskirts of Flesherton, not far from Collingwood and Owen Sound. Bill told me that he had a neighbour who carved birds and thought he'd be an interesting story.

Peter "Woody" Woodward was born a Cockney in London, England in 1938. As a youngster, he and his family survived the Blitz of World War II, spending a considerable amount of time underground in the Notting Hill Gate tube station. Woody told me that after each bombing had ended and it was safe to go back up to the streets, he and his chums would go looking for pieces of schrapnel which they'd trade amongst themselves for marbles. One day, after their next-door neighbour's house was blown away, they knew it was time to move. With his dad away at sea serving with the Royal Navy, Woody, his mom and grandmother moved south to the Cornwall and Devonshire area. All through these early years, young Woody wittled with wood. When he grew up, Woody became a surgical instrument maker. In 1957, he decided to come to Canada. There was no employment in that trade here, so he took a position with McDonnell Douglas Aircraft in Malton. For twenty-nine years he worked hard, eventually ending up as management in Human Resources. Then, he was let go, downsizing they called it. I asked Woody how it made him feel? "Well Terry, it was pretty devastating," he said. "It took me quite a while to get over it. Took about three months."

He was still young, early fifties. "Who'd hire him?" he thought. Drawing from a love he'd had as a boy, Woody started to carve birds. The day I was there he was carving the head of a Great Blue Heron. All his carvings are to size. "The most critical part of the carving I would say would be the head," said Woody. "If you get the head completed, about fifty percent of that bird is actually finished." Woody told me that a carver can only make one or two small mistakes on the face, but can make thirty to forty on the body before it becomes noticeable. In 1992, he made his first sale. He took thirty-six carved songbirds to a home show in neighbouring Dundalk and sold thirty of them. Not bad for a beginner. Popular sellers are his small birds like the chickadees. I asked him why he chose to carve songbirds. "It's interesting, Terry, because I've carved ducks, loons and many other birds, but songbirds, there's such a wide variety of them. I can keep them small and it's within the pocketbook of the average person."

The shy saw artist herself, Mary Jo Pinder, on Garafraxa Street in
Durham.

SHY SAW ARTIST

Global's labour reporter Bill Trbovich is married to Carolynne McKechnie of Durham. Quite often they'll drive up to Grey County where they have a country retreat near Priceville, or over to visit Carolynne's mother in Durham itself. Bill has always been a great source of story ideas for both himself and for me. Sometimes he finds them in their local paper, the *Durham Chronicle.* After one such visit, Bill gave me a name and telephone number of an artist. He told me that he hadn't met her, but had seen her work. She paints on old saw blades that hang on the walls of her sister's and brother-in-law's restaurant. Over the past few years I've recorded the lifestyle of many Ontario artists, some self-assured, others self-promoters. There are a few who have made it into the big time with agents and a staff to handle their work, but Mary Jo Pinder was none of those. This talented, and extremely shy artist relied on her paintings being discovered through word of mouth.

Mary Jo doesn't let moss grow under her feet. She claims she's part gypsy, always travelling, always on the move. I was fortunate to get hold of her after Bill Trbovich gave me her telephone number. She had recently returned home to Pinder's Mountain to live in her parents' cottage at the back of their property which she had converted into a home and studio. The self-taught artist was born in the northern Ontario town of Espanola. The walls of her parents A-frame cabin were covered with her paintings. Mary Jo was inspired by native Canadian art from an early age. "This is my impression of the Mohawk clan," she said. "It shows the wolf, bear and the turtle. The eagle is watching over them." She also paints on fabric. A denim jacket she was working on bore the head of an American eagle. Her fabric painting is wearable and washable.

Mary Jo's getting a positive reputation for her charming folk-art paintings on old saw blades. She was nearing completion on a huge circular saw that depicted her father's construction company. It was a scene of his business, the title painted at the top saying, "End of an Era." After thirty-eight years in the building industry, her dad was retiring and Mary Jo was painting him a keepsake.

She went on to show me a handsaw that she'd painted for her mother. It was a painting of the farm where her mom had grown up. "People bring me old saws that they find in their barns or attics," she said. "I paint their house on them or any other subject they would like." When Mary Jo finishes a piece of art, she takes it to Sue and Doug's restaurant in Durham. Called the Uptown Revue, it's become her gallery and her sister Sue Fogal, her agent. The family is always delighted to see Auntie Jo when she comes to town, especially her two-year-old nephew Chancey. This little guy was born prematurely weighing a pound and a half and, through love and the miracles of science, he's a normal, healthy little boy. The walls of the two dining rooms are Mary Jo's display areas. It took three men to hoist a circular sawblade onto the wall; it depicted nearby McGowan Falls. On another wall, a painting of Knechtel's grist mill is painted on a smaller circular sawblade.

It's almost impossible to beat the hospitality of people in the rural parts of the province. I was about to order my dinner in their restaurant when Sue said she wouldn't hear of it. Sue said that she had a big roast cooking in the apartment above and invited me to join them for dinner. It was fabulous. To top it off, the phone rang from downstairs; some of the regulars wanted Doug to bring down his guitar. When dinner was finished, we joined the guests downstairs for some honest-to-goodness fun. This was a fantastic ending to a great day.

Artist Bob Heard painted the Stouffvile Railway Station as it was in its
heyday.

RAILWAY ARTIST

Watercolourist Bob Heard and the Ministry of Canadian Heritage have one thing in common: they're both into preserving our old railway stations. In honour of Heritage Day, which took place February 21st, 1994, the Minister of Canadian Heritage, the Honourable Michel Dupuy, announced the designation of forty-five heritage railway stations. These designations are made under the Heritage Railway Stations Protection Act. Under this legislation, no railway company may remove, destroy, alter, or in any way dispose of a heritage railway station under its control without the Government of Canada's approval. As of February, 1994, there are now 131 heritage railway stations across Canada protected under the Act.

In his own way, St. Catharines' native Bob Heard is also involved in preservation. Bob's contribution is his wonderful watercolour paintings of old Ontario railway stations. He brings them to life by painting them as they were in their heyday. "I've always lived within a mile of a railroad, no matter where in Ontario I've lived," Bob said, "whether it's been in Windsor or London, Waubaushene or Toronto, Scarborough or in Stouffville. It's been about fifty years now and it's just constantly hearing the whistles and the horns of the trains going by. I've never been far away from the railway tracks." A printer by trade, Bob still works part-time for a print shop in Markham. "People think I'm kind of semi-retired because I paint pictures five or six days a week," he said, "but it doesn't really work out like that. Some days I put in ten to twelve hours and actually work harder than when I was punching a clock at the print shop. Financially, it's a little scary, but I'm having more fun and enjoying myself."

Bob doesn't want to be pigeon holed as strictly a railway artist, although that seems to be the direction his work is going. He had a great admiration for the late nostalgic railway painter Wentworth Folkin who passed away in 1993. I must admit that I was impressed with the works of this self-taught artist. Bob and I were both born in 1942, and, as we chatted over coffee, we came to the conclusion that, in our early fifties, both of our careers seemed to be going in the right direction.

The Comeback (1992) by sports artist Dan Parry

SPORTS ARTIST

Global's Sports Director Jim Tatti called me into his office to show me a couple of framed and autographed sports illustrations on his wall. He told me that his nephew, his sister's son, had drawn them.

I met Dan Parry in June of '93. The twenty seven-year-old Burlington artist had just formed a company with two marketing partners called Classic Sports Art. *Classic Alomar* was Dan's first drawing to receive the go-ahead, not only from Roberto Alomar, but also from his agent and the Toronto Blue Jays organization. It was also endorsed and licensed by Major League Baseball itself. Dan was paid the highest compliment when Roberto said it was the first artwork he's seen that really looked like him.

The Comeback is Dan's second illustration of Roberto. It's a lifelike drawing of the baseball player, as he leads the Toronto Blue Jays to an eleventh-inning victory against the Oakland A's in game four of the 1992 American League Championship Series.

Dan's company keeps the limited-edition prints to just under a thousand. Both the athlete and the artist sign each individual print. With his specialized technique of combining pencil, ink, and airbrush, Dan strives for realism in all his drawings. When I was visiting in his studio, he was putting the finishing touches on a portrait of the Toronto Maple Leafs' Doug Gilmore.

"I've always been a sports fan," said Dan, "and the thing about doing sports people like Roberto Alomar and Felix Potvin is that you really get involved in the game. Whether it be baseball or hockey, it becomes a very personal thing. After I've spent a month and a half drawing a sports personality, I don't take it too kindly when someone says they're not that great or they're not playing that well. It becomes a very, very personal thing to me. Also, it's pretty hard not to be a fan after being forced to watch my uncle Jim on *Sportsline* every night. Actually, Uncle Jim's been a great inspiration to me."

Just as a footnote: Dan's uncle Jim is Bob McAdorey's son-in-law. Jim's married to Bob's darlin' daughter Colleen.

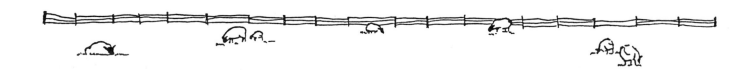

RAKU POTTER

Raku is a five hundred-year-old pottery technique involving a very rapid glaze-firing cycle. Japanese, Korean and Chinese potters used this method to produce their treasured tea bowls used in the Zen tea ceremony. I'd never seen Raku, let alone heard of it, until I went to northern Ontario in the summer of '94. There I witnessed first-hand, Bonnie Borden, a raku potter, at work. Bonnie lives with her husband Earl in a fabulous log home they built for themselves on the shore of Kenogami Lake. Bonnie's home and studio is just a few miles to the west of Swastika, near Kirkland Lake. Except for a fifteen-year stint working for Molson's Brewery in Toronto, Bonnie has always lived in this area. The mother of two is self-taught, although she's taking summer courses to earn credits towards her masters in fine arts.

In her studio, she starts her pots in the traditional way by plopping a lump of soft, damp clay onto her electric potter's wheel. After she's finished creating there, her pieces are trimmed and bisque fired before glazing. Bonnie uses metal oxides such as copper, cobalt, and iron in her glazes to help produce the lustre surface that her work obtains. When the glaze has dried, she takes her pottery outside to the raku kiln shed. Raku firing was introduced to North America at the beginning of this century. Inside the kiln the temperature reaches eleven hundred degrees celsius or eighteen hundred degrees farenheit. Once the kiln temperature has reached the desired level and the glaze has melted, Bonnie removes the pieces from the kiln with metal tongs. Each piece is placed in a pit which is covered with organic material such as sawdust or newspaper. When the red hot pot comes in contact with the organic material, it immediately ignites. Bonnie quickly covers the pottery with a metal pail which smothers the flames and prevents oxygen from the atmosphere getting in. It's the reduction of oxygen that blackens the clay and brings out the luster in the glaze.

"One of the difficulties of being an artist in the north is the marketing of one's product," she told me. "We don't have the exposure to the big craft sales and centres that they do in the south. Something I tell my husband Earl is that I've never worked so hard for so little but enjoyed it so much." Raku is very popular with artists in the warmer climates, especially in the southwestern United States. But here in northern Ontario, where the winters can be quite severe, Bonnie Borden is somewhat of a pioneer.

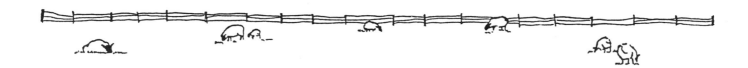

THE PORCELAIN WALTZ

As I travel this wonderful province of ours, the car radio has become my constant companion. CBC Radio is like an old friend because I can receive it anywhere. Normally on Saturday mornings I try to catch *The Max Ferguson Show* while I'm working at my desk at home. I hear it on CBC FM between 9 and 10:30 a.m. On this particular Saturday morning, during the fall of '94, I was in my automobile when I heard Max Ferguson say: "Well I finally got this gentleman's name correct, thanks to a letter he wrote me: Donald McGeough in Brantford, Ontario. He comes from a place called Barrhead in Scotland and he's written a fine song about what makes Barrhead famous. It's a company called Shanks and they make just about all the toilet bowls in the world.

And now we'll listen to the composer himself, Donald McGeough, singing this song which he calls 'The Porcelain Waltz.'"

There's nobody famous or even well known,
From the town where I grew up in and proud to call home.
There's just an old factory sits on the banks,
By Levern clear waters, that factory Shanks.
I know you will ask me, what's in a name?
In Europe it's known from Belgium to Spain.
In Vatican City, the heartbeat of Rome,
Where even his Holiness sits on your throne.
To this famous company we must give thanks,
If you're European, you're a pee'in in Shanks.

IF YOU'RE EUROPEAN.....
YOU'RE A PEE'IN IN SHANKS.

SHANKS   SHANKS   SHANKS   SHANKS

Culbert.

That's only the first verse to Donald's song. I loved it and, when the song ended, Max repeated the singing composer's name and the city where he'd penned his composition. Our newsroom has telephone books for most cities in Ontario and I was able to locate and call Donald who agreed to do a story with me. When I asked if he had any pictures of his hometown or Shanks' factory, he said no, but, if I wasn't in a big rush to do the story, he'd send for some. In the meantime he mailed me his recording. A few weeks later, Donald rang me up to say that the pictures had arrived from a friend of his in Barrhead and he was ready to do the story. In a suburban Brantford home, I met Donald and his lovely wife Brenda. He was not the boisterous sort of man that I had conjured up in my mind. If anything, Donald was a bit shy. Donald and Brenda met in Barrhead and eventually the young woman from Paisely would wed the man she'd taken a shine to in a bowling alley. Donald is a carpenter and had served his apprenticeship in the village of Neilston, near Barrhead. His brother David was the only family member that worked at Shanks, making brass fittings. In 1974, the McGeough's and their five-year-old daughter Angela moved to Canada. The couple both work for the Brantford General Hospital, he as a carpenter and she as a purchasing supervisor. I didn't meet Angela, but I was told by the proud parents that she was engaged to be married.

"The Porcelain Waltz" is just one of five songs that Donald composed for his first recording, titled *Land of the Western Sky*, on their own independent label. They funded the project entirely on their own. With musician friends donating their time and talent, it still cost the McGeoughs six thousand dollars. The recording also includes songs such as "Lancashire Lads" and "Dumbarton's Drums." The title track, "Land of the Western Sky," was written by Donald and is about the uncertainty of emigrating to Canada. "Homeland," another of his compositions, is an affectionate backward look to his native Caledonia. The singing stonemason Bobby Watt made Donald's "Homeland" the title track on his recording a couple years ago.

In 1982, Brenda and Donald founded The Brantford Folk Club, a non-profit organization that meets every other Friday from September till June. The club provides space and a sound system for local talent, including Donald. Every so often they bring special guests in, like Dougie MacLean from Scotland, Four Men and a Dog, an Irish group based in Belfast, Eric Bogle, a Scot living in Australia, my friend the singing Scottish stonemason Bobby Watt and Canadian folksinger Garnet Rogers. "Brenda and I started the folk club," said Donald, "because there was a void in our lives when we moved to Canada. We were missing a lot of the music, particularly the Scottish music."

To complete my story on Donald, I called Li Robbins, the producer of *The Max Ferguson Show* and asked her if it would be possible to shoot a few scenes of Max in the studio? A few days later she called back to say it was okay. This was fantastic news, as Max's portion was an important element to my story. On the designated day, I arrived at the new CBC Toronto complex in time to have lunch and a mini-tour with my dear friend Joe Coté. He's host of *Ontario Morning*. Then it was up to Studio 204 to meet Li, Max, and broadcaster Sheila Rogers. With the assistance of Bruce Barnett, the show's technician, I was able to record what I needed, including Max re-enacting those words I'd heard over the airwaves many weeks earlier.

Culbert.

THE MUSIC OF COW AND SOW

The headline read: "Cow and Sow Farm in Harmony." The article went on to describe how two farmers get together to play Mozart, Bach, and Brahms. David Murray is a dairy farmer and Dominik Franken raises hogs. Well, after reading this in the "Farm Life" section of *Farm and Country,* I just had to pay them a visit. I met David at the pre-arranged time on his Perth County farm. He milks a herd of thirty-six cows, half Holstein, the other eighteen Jersey. He owns the cattle and the milk quota, but rents the barn from his in-laws. It was a magnificent summer's morning as I took pictures of David and his young son herding the cows from the barn out toward the pasture. When I'd taken all the pictures I required, David invited me home for lunch. His wife had gone to a lot of trouble preparing the meal, although she told me she hadn't. The food was wonderful and reminded me of the times I'd spent around the kitchen table at my grandparents farm near Lucan. After lunch, David went off to scrub up for that afternoon's musical engagement at the Ritz-Lutheran Villa in Mitchell.

At the Villa, I met Dominik; in the music business he's known as Sow. Dominik has a 240-acre farm near Mitchell and after the concert was over we drove out there to get him in action. Dominik runs a farrow-to-finish swine operation and grows cash crops. At one time the two men farmed along the same concession road, but didn't know each other.

Dominik began violin studies at the age of eight in his native Germany. Six years later, his music teacher gave him a viola, which sparked a lifelong love affair with that melodious instrument. As a teenager, he travelled the world as part of the German Youth Orchestra. David began piano studies as a child and studied music for two years at Wilfred Laurier University in Waterloo.

When the pair first met, they had misgivings about whether they were compatible as musical partners. "We didn't expect too much from each other," said Dominik, "but when David hit the piano keys and I drew the bow across the viola, it was magic." David went on to say: "After we'd practised for a couple of weeks, we really began enjoying it. Then we had the idea . . . why not give a concert?" The rest, as they say, is history, and they've been doing concerts ever since.

With the assistance of page-turner Brad Carew, Cow and Sow began their concert for the residents of Ritz-Lutheran Villa. Because of their farm commitments, it's a rare for an audience to hear the men play during the summer months. They normally schedule their concerts for early spring or late fall when the farm work is less demanding. As they played the works of the romantic composers, I watched the seniors' faces. Some sat with their eyes closed, others sat with tilted head, a smile upon their face. Everyone in the room that day listened and enjoyed the music. When you first hear their stage name, Cow and Sow, you conjure up a picture in your mind of a couple of buffoons dressed in costume. But not so with this pair. They were professional musicians all the way, including the conservative suits they wore. I could have listened to them for hours.

IONOSPHERIC SOUNDWALK

I wasn't quite sure what to expect when I first heard about a character in London, Ontario, who collects strange sounds from the upper atmosphere and assembles them into a form of musical symphony. When I finally tracked down Chris Meloche, he seemed quite normal to me. He wasn't speaking in tongues and I actually understood every word he said. But, would I be able to make a story of what he does? Well, my worries were for naught. Without the slightest hesitation, he took the technical jargon used in describing these sounds and put it into layman's language that even I understood.

For the visual portion of my television story, Chris and I went to Victoria Park in downtown London. Here Chris set up his equipment as he's done dozens of times before. Then he sat down on a campstool. Using a special device known as a radio receiver, a small recorder the size of a walkman, a headset and a three foot telescopic antenna, he began to listen and record. People passing by would take a second look and most gave a puzzled smile as they kept on walking. The squirrels, collecting their winter nuts, seemed to be unaware of his presence in the park. With all his equipment turned on, Chris recorded the normally inaudible electrical signals bouncing around the upper atmosphere. These are sounds of big static discharges which are much the same as pulling your socks apart after they get stuck together in the clothes dryer. These discharges are sounds caused by lightning storms in the upper atmosphere and, because they're electrical and not acoustic, we don't hear them.

After I'd taken all the scenes I required in the park, we returned to his home and studio where I photographed Chris assembling his day's work on a multi-track recording setup. He took his recorded tweeks, whistlers, and 'sferics and transformed them into what he calls nature's own symphony. 'Sferics are the sort of generic crackling and popping of electrical energy that's going on all around the world twenty-four hours a day. Tweeks are focused zaps of energy that happen amongst the 'sferics; they make a pinging sound. Whistlers are like tweeks except they're travelling very fast and the high frequencies get to you before the low frequencies. So what you hear is a descending tone, like a bomb dropping. Chris, on his very elaborate soundboard, alters the sounds with reverb, delay, and pitch, effectively creating a unique mix of art and science.

Composer Meloche calls his music from the sky "Ionospheric Soundwalk." His compositions have been broadcast by Radio France International, Radio Moscow, and Radio Budapest. Chris' exploration of radio-frequency phenomena can also be heard weekly on the University of Western Ontario's CHRW 94.7 FM Radio Western in London. Audio artist Chris Meloche turned out to be one of the most interesting subjects that I've chosen to do a story on.

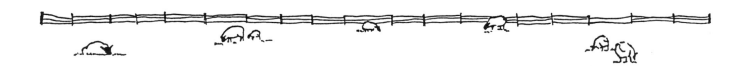

STONEMASONRY SCHOOL

In the fall of 1990, my colleague and fellow cameraman Rick Dade told me about Bobby Watt, a Scottish friend of his who had a band called Cromdale. Rick, a piper with Toronto's Metropolitan Police Band, had worked with Bobby at various functions. I did the story of Cromdale and included a few scenes of Bobby working with stone on a new home in Toronto's prestigious Bridle Path district. The burly, bearded man had come to Canada as a stonemason after apprenticing in Scotland. He'd served his time working on the majestic Brodick Castle located on the Isle of Arran where Bobby was raised. When he first arrived in this country there wasn't a big demand for his trade, so he became a Toronto policeman. He worked with the marine unit finding all kinds of goodies in the city harbour. By the time I met him, he'd given up police work and was doing well in the stone trade. The band Cromdale is no more, but Bobby Watt has soldiered on as a soloist and has done extremely well. He travels all over North America and periodically returns to his roots in Scotland to perform. Bobby's two CD's are titled *Homeland* and *C'est Watt.*

In September of '93, Bobby approached Durham College in Whitby and proposed a stonemasonry course. They loved his idea and, by the fourth of January 1994, Bobby Watt and Durham College started the first stonemasonry course in Ontario's history. "The whole thing started purely and simply because we discovered there's about 650 people working in the restoration masonry industry," Bobby said, "and probably only 50 or 60 of them really have a clue as to what they're doing." The Ontario Provincial Advisory Committee claims they need close to 300 qualified stonemasons to complete a billion dollars' worth of restoration. It would take the twenty-three real stonemasons in this province, including Bobby, one thousand years to finish the work that's needed to be done right now. The course is fifteen months long, one thousand hours in the classroom and nine months working at actual historic sites throughout Ontario. "The buildings are at a critical age where, if they aren't looked after properly from this point on," he said, "we'll lose them very, very quickly, and indeed some have already been condemned." The first class at Durham College was an interesting mix: Finbarr Sheehan is a landed immigrant from Ireland and he'd been a stone setter; David Underwood had been a bricklayer for twenty-two years. "On the first day of the course when Bobby was outlining it," said David, "it was rekindling an old flame that was in the process of dying because of the work I was involved in. I'm hoping now that I'll be able to further develop myself in the stone industry." The only woman in the class of twenty was Jennifur Ross, and, yes, that's the way she spells it. "I worked in the Toronto theatre industry for years and last year I was given a piece of soapstone for a birthday gift. After working with it I was hooked. I absolutely had to do this for the rest of my life." The fact that this course has started ensures that buildings and monuments from our past will remain for future generations. In all the stories that I've done, this one got the most response; Global news received dozens of inquiries about the stonemasonry course.

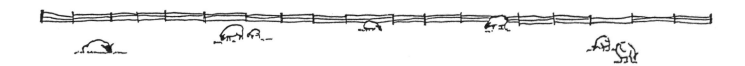

Wagon maker Delmer Hughson of Priceville, attaching a lamp to his elegant
hitch wagon.

HORSE-DRAWN WAGONS

The Durham Chronicle featured a story of a craftsman making horse-drawn wagons. "What a perfect story for television," I thought, as I clipped out the article and got the wagon maker's phone number from the long-distance operator. Delmer Hughson is a well-built, good-looking man who resembles an old-fashioned cowboy. The way he walks, talks, and dresses, you'd think he'd stepped straight out of the movie screen. Delmer grew up on a farm in Kent County and has had horses in his life as far back as he remembers. A few years ago he decided to look for greener pastures and bought himself a spread in Priceville, in the Owen Sound area. He grows a few crops on his farm, but makes his living driving an eighteen-wheeler for a Flesherton gravel pit. It's what he does in his spare time that this story is all about. Delmer is a craftsman from a bygone era, building gorgeous horse-drawn wagons in a two-car garage alongside his house where he's set up shop. The day I arrived, it was cold and raining. It was early May and, even with his woodburning stove roaring away, it was damp and chilly inside that shed. After setting up my two 600-watt lamps, I shot scenes of Delmer building a three-seat surry for a customer in Caledon East. The price for a new wagon ranges from five to fifteen thousand dollars. The self-taught wagon maker builds from scratch. Nails, screws, and bolts are hidden from view. He also does restoration work on old wagons the same time-honoured way—by hand. This whole thing began for Delmer twenty odd years ago when he restored a doctor's buggy. The first new wagon that he ever built was for a friend's wedding. The weather was still miserable as we completed shooting indoors, so I suggested that I'd return at a later date to finish the story; I still needed an interview and scenes of his prize wagon being pulled by his team of blond Tennessee mules.

It was the following month when I could return to the area. I had lined up a couple more stories and had set up an appointment with the wagon maker for the afternoon of one of those days. It was a glorious day when I arrived; the sky was a deep blue, dotted with picture-perfect clouds. Delmer went back to the barn to hitch up the mules; he'd purchased the pair from a farmer in Tennessee specifically to pull his elegant hitch wagon. The wagon that he'd built for himself was so well made that it received no appreciable damage when a friend of his flipped it on its side and dragged it during competition. Delmer drove his mules and wagon about a mile from his farm to a tree-lined dirt road where I shot my action scenes. "The wagon's basically an oak wagon, painted," he said. "I put mirrors along the front, side and back for decoration. I installed lamps on both sides and have adapted the power so that I make the electrical bulbs flicker as if they were candles. The whole wagon's pretty impressive in the darkened show ring with the spot light on it."

He shows his wagon and mules at parades and competitions, and they can be hired out for weddings. Delmer also does promotional work for Algonquin Breweries with their spokesman, former hockey great Bobby Hull. When Delmer is building a wagon, it can take him several months, and in the winter it's bone-chilling cold inside his workshop. So, why does he do it? "It's a challenge," says Delmer. "Gives me something to do with my spare time. You really feel you've done something when you see the end result. Most people are very appreciative and that gives me a real good feeling."

New Liskeard paddle maker Harry Teal. His motto: *the Teal paddle, like the Teal Duck, belongs in the water.*

PADDLE MAKER

One April afternoon an old school friend paid me a visit. Harold Frost and I had grown up together in Lucan. Harold had made a career with the Ontario Ministry of Natural Resources and the last time I saw him he was working as a forest operation technician stationed in Hearst. He took early retirement from Natural Resources and has set up his own company, Nagagami Forestry Service, in Wawa. When he came for the visit, he was accompanied by Connie and Gord Langille. Gord is with TransCanada Pipelines and the Langilles and Frosts had been neighbours in Hearst. I made the comment that I was headed for the tri-town area of Cobalt, Haileybury, and New Liskeard the following week. "If you have the time you've got to visit Harry Teal," said Gord. "He's a fine paddle maker." Tips on people and places like this give me many of my story ideas. Through the long-distance operator I tracked down paddle maker Teal.

Teal Paddles is located a few miles to the northwest of New Liskeard. The cottage industry was much larger than I had anticipated: I'd pictured Harry working alone in a shed next to his house, making possibly two canoe paddles a day. I was really surprised when I walked into the barn-shaped building and standing before me were three people all hard at work. Each person was operating a fairly large piece of power equipment. The noise was deafening and you had to shout to be heard. It turned out to be a family operation; Harry's wife Linda is an important part of the business. Using the band saw, she cuts the blanks out for the paddles, oars, and yokes. Mike Bowering, their son-in-law, apprenticed under Harry and now can do about everything. That day he was rounding an oar handle on the lathe. This oar was ash, but they also use poplar and birch.

Their quality products are sold as far away as Europe and Japan.

Harry and his family moved to the north from Welland in 1974 and for the first two years he worked with his brother-in-law in the bush. A friend of his, the originator of the Scott Canoe, asked him to make a few canoe paddles. "I wasn't doing anything at the time, so I decided to give it a try, and I've been trying ever since." said Harry. I asked him if the recession had affected his business? "I never noticed the recession. I think maybe people are settling on canoeing instead of outboard motoring and that helps me."

With the excess wood cut off the oar blade, it was time for Mike to sand and buff it before the varnish could be applied. It's a labour-intensive process and there's still a lot of handwork to be done even though they use power tools.

Harry was making yokes of cherry wood. Yokes are used by canoeists to provide a bit of comfort while carrying the canoe on their shoulders. Everything produced in this northern Ontario woodworking shop gets two coats of varnish. The trademark of a Teal duck is branded on each finished piece Harry's motto is The Teal Paddle, like the Teal duck, belongs in the water. A good feeling came over me when I realized that there are craftspeople still making quality products.

The early voyageurs used paddles to propel their freight canoes, carrying supplies and furs from one remote trading post to another. Today, a modified version of that original broad-bladed implement can be seen as canoeists paddle the lakes and streams of our vast land. So look closely the next time you see a canoeist going by and as the blade surfaces you may see a teal duck branded on it.

Two members of the famed musical Schryer family at work on St. Joseph Island. Violin maker Raymond Schryer on the left, with his younger brother, Pierre.

VIOLIN MAKER

Dave Wilson is a native of Sault Ste. Marie, Ontario. He's also a free-lance television news cameraman who occasionally works at Global. Dave told me about his cousin Raymond, a violin maker on St. Joseph Island, and thought that it would make a good lifestyle story for me. Dave was right.

It was 7:30 on a Friday morning in 1994. The August sun was rising over the St. Joseph Channel and I'd spent my second night in the cozy Hilton Beach Hotel on St. Joseph Island. This was my first visit and on Thursday I'd shot a story at Fort St. Joseph. Built by the British in the 1790s, the historic ruins are now a tourist attraction run by Parks Canada. The village of Hilton Beach is one of the larger communities on the Island and is just forty-five km from Sault Ste. Marie.

In 1992, a new business came to the village. The old Town Hall was purchased and converted into the Schryer Violin Workshop. Raymond Schryer, the owner, makes his own line of world-class violins, violas, and cellos and is a restorer of old instruments. He apprenticed in the late '70s and early '80s at the violin workshop of George Heinl and Company in Toronto.

Raymond is part of the famous Schryer Family, known throughout Canada as a Canadian fiddle legend. The family has won every major fiddling competition in Canada, and now they're able to play their wonderful music on Raymond's violins. Raymond told me that, if their father hadn't played the guitar and sung Hank Williams songs, there's a darn good chance the family would not have become involved in music. In 1993, Raymond's younger brother

Pierre joined the firm as an apprentice. In his late twenties, Pierre is an award-winning classically trained violinist. Born at the same time as his brothers Louis and Daniel, they perform as The Schryer Triplets. When I originally called to set up the story, Raymond was in Russia. He was attending the Tchaikovsky International Violin Making Competition in Moscow. International jury members selected and presented him with a bronze for his cello and a Lauret diploma for his viola. This event is like the Olympics for instrument makers and included two hundred competitors. Raymond's secret to success in violin making is his respect for the standards set by famed Italian violin maker Antonius Stradivarius. The Master's three-centuries-old instruments still haven't been surpassed for tone, power or form. "I make my violins and cellos to Stradivarius' measurements and designs," said Raymond. Stradivarius used spruce wood for the tops and maple for the backs. They were quarter cut and air dried." Tapping the back of the instrument with his finger, Raymond got a bonk, bonk, bonk sound. "You get this kind of bright sound from that quality of wood," he said. "Stradivarius calibrated the measurements for thickness to the tenth of a millimetre." Raymond tunes his backs to "G" and the tops to "F," giving him a good sound. It takes Raymond about two hundred hours to make one violin. It's a type of work definitely not recommended for those short on patience.

At a recent concert in Michigan, Raymond asked famed violinist Itzak Perlman to try his instrument after the performance. He agreed, he played, he was impressed with Raymond's craftsmanship.

STRATFORD CANDY MA...

My wife Donna and I were out grocery shopping when CBC Radio reporter Jane Antoniac told the story of a family run candy store in Stratford. Jane was interviewing the candy maker about Valentine's Day. Donna, as thin as she is, is a chocoholic and a superb candy maker herself. She suggested that the candy maker would make a good television story. When we got home, I telephoned the operator in Stratford and told her about the radio story and that I missed the candy maker's name. "No problem sir," she said, "that would be Rheo Thompson's Candy Shop and you can reach him at area code 519-271-6910. Their chocolates are fantastic . . . they're the best."

Visiting Stratford, you'd be hard pressed to find any of the twenty-seven thousand residents that couldn't direct you to Rheo Thompson's Candy Shop. The Festival City is blessed with a wonderful candy maker who began his career at the age of eighteen. Rheo served his apprenticeship under Olin Brown in a family firm that started in that city in the 1800s. When the Brown candy store was sold, Rheo stayed on, but the new owners weren't the same. Eventually, with ten years of making candy under his belt, he went out on his own, manufacturing from home. He sold his products at the Stratford Farmers Market. His insistence on quality was quickly recognized and it soon became evident that he needed more space. After purchasing a building at 26 Brunswick Street, Rheo and his wife Sally have never stopped expanding. From their tiny beginnings, they now operate in close to seven thousand square feet.

Depending upon the season, the Thompsons employ ten to eighteen people. Their busiest period is Christmas, followed by Easter, then Valentine's. Candy for weddings has become very popular. "Traditionally, brides used to give away wedding cake," Rheo said, "but today we find a lot of them coming into our store and buying packages of chocolate. We also add the service of wrapping the chocolates in the same colour as the bridesmaids' dresses. This has become very popular and seems to go on twelve months of the year." When I was there, they were getting ready for Easter. Rich chocolate swirled in the blender. Ken Lowe pumped it into Easter bunny moulds. Ken apprenticed in the art of candy making under Rheo. On the second floor, Lucie Penney was filling boxes with an assortment of chocolates. She hand picked the light and dark candies as they rotated in front of her on a machine that resembled a small Ferris wheel. The employees are never stuck doing the same chore, but rotate through the various operations including selling at the front counter. For the true chocolate lover, the store is where it all begins. If you love chocolate, you'll find it hard not to buy some when the aroma first hits you.

Rheo Thompson's best-selling candy is his Mint Smoothie. They make thirty thousand pounds or fifteen tons of them a year. I brought a box home to Donna and, after sampling her first Smoothie, she could tell why they were the customers' favorite. I took Donna and her mother to Stratford to visit the store and to picnic by the Avon River. I now have a standing order from my wife: if I'm within a few miles of the shop, I'm not to come home without a box of Mint Smoothies.

WEIGHTLIFTING SHOES

Global's *News at Noon* anchor Loretta Sullivan recently asked me to give her brother Mike a call. Mike Sullivan told me about a shoemaker in the west end of Toronto who not only fixes broken and worn footwear, but is the only craftsman in world making custom shoes for weight-lifters. It turns out that Mike Czifra of Mike's European Expert Shoe Service has a vested interest in making them. A few years ago, Mike was watching one of his grandsons lifting weights in competition. "He was wearing running shoes," said Mike, "he's wobbling. I'm scared he's not going to be able to hold the weight. Well, he did, but after the competition I take away the shoes and put a new wood heel and sole on them. Five weeks later he's able to make a good clean five kilo extra." From that first pair of shoes, word spread and now his custom, handmade shoes are on athletes all across Canada. As a matter of fact, he even received an order from a powerlifter for a pair of size sixteens. From his compact workshop adjoining his store, Mike constructs weight-lifters' shoes with wooden heels and soles of rubber to prevent slipping. Mike began his career in Budapest, Hungary at the age of thirteen. He still works sixty hours a week, even after his heart went through a triple by-pass.

Not many years ago, Mike sponsored his stepson Steve Sandor and his family to come to Canada. Steve is a former Hungarian weightlifting champion and now he's the trainer to his sons Akos and Balazs. Three times a week, the family trains together at the Jewish Community Sports Centre in North York. This is the only facility in the Toronto area with proper olympic-style platforms that withstand the weights when they come crashing down. Most nights you'll find Grandpa Mike at the gym with his family. He gives them moral support and is constantly checking out their feet. They all wear Mike's shoes. Steve Sandor missed the 1984 Olympics in Los Angeles because of a communist boycott. Now he would like nothing better than to see his own dream come true through his sons participating in the Olympics of 2000. Naturally they'll both be wearing their grandpa Mike's custom-made weight-lifting shoes.

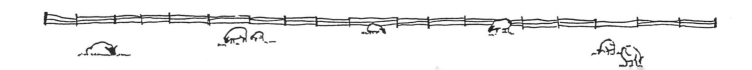

Photograph courtesy of The Collingwood Skiff Project

Nahma II, the last existing Watts Skiff. The twenty-six-foot-long, two-masted, double-ended sailboat was owned by the late Ken Jones of Toronto.

WATTS SKIFF

The early settlers found that Georgian Bay was one of the most abundant fishing grounds in the New World. Surrounded by forests, the town of Collingwood made an ideal location for building fishing boats and in the early 1800s, quite a number of small boatbuilding companies sprang up. One of those was the Watts Boatbuilding Company, started in 1860 by an Irish boatbuilder named William Watts. For the next eighty-three years, there were literally hundreds of Watts boats built in the Collingwood harbour and sold all over North America. The most popular Watts fishing boat was his skiff, a beamy boat that was very stable in rough water. Because it drew only eighteen inches of water, it could fish near the shoals and in other shallow areas. It had fifty percent more sail than other boats of its size, enabling it to outrun stormy weather. Today, only one original Watts Skiff survives, and it's in pretty sad shape. *Nahma II* sits on a cradle at Ashbridges Bay Yacht Club in Toronto.

I must tell you an interesting fact that I didn't have for my television feature. When I picked up the corrected pages of this manuscript from my editor, John Stevens, he informed me that his great-grandfather, Sir Edmund Walker, had *Nahma II* built in 1922 as a replacement for his *Nahma I*, also a Watts Skiff. *Nahma II* was similar to her predecessor except that she was twenty-six feet long—two feet shorter. Her spars and rigging were adapted from those of *Nahma I,* and sails were re-cut for her smaller size; a total of 455 square feet. Both *Nahma I* and *II* plied the waters of Lake Simcoe from De Grassi Point on Cooks Bay.

In 1937 *Nahma II* was sold to Stanley Bâby, whose father was an old lake skipper. He turned the skiff over to the Sea Scouts in Port Credit, who used her as a training ship. Their sailing instructor, Ken Jones, purchased it from the Sea Cadets in 1952. The double-ended fishing boat was his pride and joy. Ken raced it along Lake Ontario for forty years, never losing a race. Mr. Jones passed away in June of 1994 and one of his final wishes was for *Nahma II* to be returned to Collingwood, to be housed forever in the Collingwood Museum. He wanted to be the last person to sail her.

I heard about this interesting piece of Canadian history from a group calling themselves The Collingwood Skiff Project. Dedicated volunteers interested in preserving Collingwood's marine heritage, they were building a replica of the original Watts Skiff in a vacant service station that the town had loaned them. Here I witnessed a level of community co-operation, spirit and pride that's almost a thing of the past. "The spirit of donating and scrounging lumber has been fantastic," said Gord Hanson, project chairman. "Pretty well everything, including C-clamps and 1623 pounds of lead we're going to use as ballast was donated." One of the volunteers was Tom Ridding, a retired naval architect and boat designer in the Collingwood Shipyards. Constructing a boat as they built it a hundred years ago is not easy. The group is grateful to the National Museum of Science and Technology for allowing them to use the "lines." Tom translated the lines into building plans before the actual vessel could be started. Jeff Laws, an Owen Sound cabinetmaker, was the main builder. In nautical terms Jeff would be the ship's joiner. Students from the woodworking class of Collingwood Collegiate became involved. The Collingwood Skiff Project committee hopes that their replica will sail for the next 110 years. It's intended to be a salute to the boatbuilding and shipbuilding heritage that made Collingwood famous the world over.

On Victoria Day, May 22, 1995, *Endurable I* was christened and side-launched at Sunset Point in Collingwood.

BOOMERANG MAN

Mention the word boomerang and what comes to mind? A flat V-shaped stick invented in Australia that comes back when you throw it. Right? Only partially. It does get its name from down under. It's the aboriginal word for wind, *boomeri*, but the oldest known boomerang wasn't found in Australia as you'd expect; it was located in Poland, and it's approximately twenty three thousand years old.

The only manufacturer of boomerangs in Canada is John Cryderman of Chatham. His factory is located in the cramped basement of his home. It's a one-man operation. "For many years there have been manufacturers that have made boomerangs," he told me. "Unfortunately people became discouraged because they didn't work properly. The same principles that make an airplane fly also apply to the boomerang. For the past ten years I've been studying what makes airplanes fly and applying that aeronautical knowledge to my boomerangs." John, who's also a promoter, tried to have the 1993 World Boomerang Championships held in Chatham, on the large playing field behind the Kent County Municipal Building. But at the last moment they were cancelled for safety reasons by city officials. Sixteen countries would have participated. As part of a promotion for the games, John made a set of Royal Boomerangs as a gift for Prince Charles. They were valued at twenty thousand dollars. John showed me the thank-you letter that he'd received from Buckingham Palace.

After we'd finished shooting a sequence of John making his boomerangs, we headed out to a playing field so that I could get some action shots. The weather had turned wet and windy and the boomerang just wouldn't come back. I asked John if he knew of anyone near Toronto that could throw it for me. Unfortunately he didn't.

Using my old noggin, I rang up Dean Ross, a New Zealand friend. He put me in touch with Willy Faraday, another New Zealander. Willy had an Australian mate named Rosscoe Heilmann who'd been throwing the V-shaped stick since his Boy Scout days in Adelaide. With the weather being the chief factor, Rosscoe and I lined up a morning so that I could get the visuals needed to finish my story. It rained. We ended up trying a number of different dates, but always the weather turned on us. Finally on the fifth try we made it. "As you can see, there's about a five or ten km breeze today," said Rosscoe. "You throw it into the breeze, but you throw it at two o'clock. In other words, the breeze is here and you tend to throw it out that way, which brings it there and then straight back to you, if you're fortunate." Remember the old song: "My boomerang won't come back, my boomerang won't come back, I've waved the thing all over the place, I'm a big disgrace. . . . "

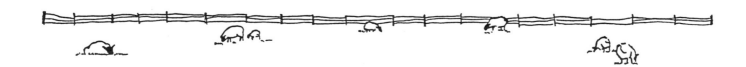

BLACKSMITH OF ARGYLE

The Victoria County hamlet of Argyle is located where County Roads 15 and 8 meet up with Highway 46. On the northwest corner of that intersection is a large, white clapboard building. When the weather is warm, the sliding door is open and this is the sound you'll hear coming from within: "clang, clang, clang." That sound is being made by a blacksmith as he hammers a piece of red hot iron on his anvil.

Working away in his dimly lit and cluttered shop is a bearded bear of a man called Lloyd Johnston. Using a coal forge along with hammers and tongs, you'd swear you'd stepped back into the nineteenth century. "The family's been blacksmithing for five generations," said Lloyd. "The family came to Canada in 1831 from County Tyrone in Northern Ireland, and we've been blacksmiths in this country ever since."

I came across Lloyd in a very unusual way. I had left home that mid-April morning to do a story on fish that were supposed to be spawning. It turned out they weren't and, not wanting to go back empty-handed, I paid a visit to Gary Goldsworthy in nearby Beaverton. I'd met Gary and his family a few years earlier when I was Bill Bramah's main cameraman. Gary is a maker of model ships. I told Gary of my plight and asked him if he knew of any craftspeople in the area who might make a good story. He told me about the blacksmith of Argyle, but wasn't sure if Lloyd would do it. "A bit shy is our Lloyd," said Gary, "but let's pay him a visit anyway."

Lloyd was great and offered to doing the story with me right then and there. It turned out that he had a big project on the go, refurbishing the gates to the entrance of the Royal Botanical Garden in Hamilton. He'd gone over with his truck and brought the whole gate back to his shop. Parts of the gate were so badly worn that Lloyd had to remake sections. I watched him heat and form some leaves. These gates were originally designed and constructed sixty years ago by a blacksmith called Fredrick J. Flatman. The top portion of the main gate is made of Swedish wrought iron and weighs almost half a tonne. Although the gate was originally completed in 1932, it wasn't erected at the Hamilton gardens until 1954.

"I was educated to be an electrical engineer," said Lloyd, "but when I graduated, I found that working with iron was more interesting to me. My schooling hasn't been a total waste because some of the principles of engineering have been a help. I just find that working with my hands is more satisfying than sitting behind a desk."

In our high-tech world, it was a pleasure to meet and watch Lloyd work. He spends a good deal of his time doing custom pieces for pioneer museums and historical sites. He's done structural steel work on the movie set of *Agnes of God* and also on the television series *Road to Avonlea*. Lloyd hasn't had to give out business cards in the past few years, because he's got a great reputation as a blacksmith.

Photographs: June Chambers

Bruce Chambers of Bond Head uses a wooden mallet and a froe as he prepares chair leg blanks from a trunk of hard maple.

A finished comb-back Windsor Chair.

WINDSOR CHAIR MAKER

I was enroute to Port Carling to do a story about an island that was for sale. On Highway 400, just before the Bradford turnoff, I was radioed by the newsroom that a storm had moved into the Muskoka area. That meant that I wouldn't be able to take a boat out on Lake Rosseau to get to the island. As I swung around the cloverleaf to head back, I noticed an antique store next to the Huskey Service Centre. Always in the market for unsual beer bottles or cans for my collection, I asked the chap in charge if there were any interesting artists or craftspeople in the area. "By golly, there is," he told me. "There's a young man that makes Windsor chairs the old-fashioned way over in Bond Head." That's all I needed to know. The Windsor Chair has been around since the late 1600s. The well-to-do English originally used it as a garden chair and it was often painted dark green to blend in with the foliage. The Colonists brought them to North America and used them as everyday furniture. They became known as the common-man's chair.

Bruce Chambers calls his business Circa 1850. His workshop was once the Bond Head Loyal Orange Lodge. The twenty seven-year-old makes Windsor Chairs exactly as the originals were made. Using a wooden mallet and a froe, Bruce fashions chair leg blanks out of the trunk of a hard maple. At this point the wood is green, but, as it dries, the shrinkage eliminates the use of nails and screws. Bruce's chairs are made from a variety of woods. He uses hard maple for the legs, white ash for the back and spindles, and pine for the seat. To be historically accurate, the pine seat must be of one piece.

Using a draw knife, the chair seat is sculpted, and the corners are chamfered off. A veining chisel outlines the area between the spindel holes and the section where one's derriere sits. With the chair seat placed on the floor and his feet holding it firmly, a round-edged hand cutting tool called an adze is used to dress the timber, to rough out the seat bottom. Bruce finishes off the seat, using a half-round-edge tool called a scorp, drawing it towards him to smooth the rough surface left by the adze.

His interest in chairs began at an early age. His parents would attend auction sales and periodically bring home a chair. When I had the pleasure of visiting him during the summer of '91, he had already made well over two hundred chairs in his seven-year career. Bruce guarantees his Windsor Chairs for at least one hundred years from loosening or breaking under normal use.

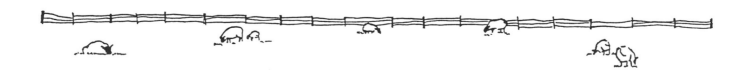

CROQUET MALLET MAKER

The origins of croquet remain clouded in obscurity. It's thought that the game began in France during the 1400s. Then it's said that croquet moved across the sea to Ireland. It finally ended up in England about a hundred and fifty years ago.

As a youngster I spent many summer afternoons playing the game with my cousins Campbell, Brian, and Wayne on the front lawn of our grandparents' farm northwest of Lucan. It's defined as an outdoor game, played by driving wooden balls through a series of wire arches or hoops by means of a long-handled mallet.

Croquet seemed to fade away for many years, but there is definitely a resurgence in its popularity these days with the forming of Croquet Canada in 1987. There are over thirty organized clubs throughout the country and universities are introducing the game into their varsity programs.

Near the Northumberland County village of Brighton, I met Don Oakley, a woodturner by trade. A few years ago he turned his talents to making custom croquet mallets. His one-man cottage industry is set up in an old dairy barn. Don has set his sights on outfitting new croquet clubs.

"It all started when a friend of mine came to me with a set of croquet mallets that had been brutalized over the past couple of summers," said Don. "He asked me for a replacement set that would be more durable." After researching how the mallets should have been made, Don built his friend a new set. That was the beginning of his own company called Oakley Woods. He now produces a variety of mallets, including a backyard version. It has a hard maple head with a walnut sight line. For the tournament player, he machines a synthetic head from a polyethylene rod. For the traditional player, Don makes a square mallet using Mexican Xatalox wood. It's bound in brass to prevent the corners from splitting. "The square head is used so you can get in for that tighter shot at the wicket," said Don. Then he jokingly added, "Some players believe it's square design means that they can leave it standing when they go off the court to get a martini or a gin and tonic. It means that they won't have to bend over for it when they return to play."

I caught up with Don a year later at the prestigious Toronto Cricket Club. As the only manufacturer of complete croquet sets, he spends many weekends during the summer travelling to interclub tournaments and national events promoting his product.

Lynda Mannik began creating her amazing
sweaters to make people feel attractive and
special, as well as cozy and comfortable.

ORIGINAL SWEATERS

Just as the cooler weather was arriving in the fall of '91, my friend and Global reporter Paul Dalby told me about a lady in Lakefield who makes gorgeous original sweaters. She's an old friend of Wendy Lang-Dalby, Paul's wife.

Lynda Mannik began making her unique garments because she wanted to create sweaters using only the finest of fibres. Sheep's wool has been used for clothing since 2000 B.C. Unlike fur, cotton, silk or linen, wool is taken from a live animal and is classified as a "living fibre." Born in Toronto of Estonian and British parents, Lynda's mother taught her to knit at an early age. She began by knitting for her Barbie dolls; then, as the years passed by, she designed all kinds of clothing for herself, her family, and her girl-friends. She has drawn all her life, has worked in stained-glass, and has a degree in design from George Brown College in Toronto. Today, married and with child, she lives in the village of Lakefield just north of Peterborough. She calls her studio Mannik Designs. Using her talents as a graphic designer and her skills as a knitter, she creates garments that surround the wearer, making them feel as if they are immersed in a work of art. Lynda is inspired by her natural surroundings, aboriginal heritage, and the rugged countryside.

After she designs a sweater, she knits the front, back and sleeves on a small hand-knitting machine, powered only by the human body. Following a graphed chart, the different coloured strands of wool are laid across the needles, using up to sixty strands on one row, depending on the pattern.

"All my life I've created clothing," said Lynda, "but I didn't want to create clothing just for materialistic reasons. I wanted to create clothing for spiritual reasons. When I started to think about the spiritual things behind clothing, I realized that all through history people have used clothing to celebrate their culture, their tradition, and dance. When I thought about Canadian clothing, the only thing that was of any spiritual nature came from our First Nations people."

Lynda's designs range from native Canadian to Canadian plants and wildlife. One sweater depicts the first Canadian stamp which was published in 1851 and known as "the three-penny beaver." Other designs show the Petroglyph symbols that can be found on the rocks just north of Lakefield. It sometimes surprises her that men choose sweaters for themselves that she had designed with a woman in mind.

Weaving in the loose ends on a sweater or vest is only one of the reasons why it takes Lynda twenty five to forty hours to complete her original sweaters. She guarantees the workmanship of each garment for a lifetime. With proper care, each piece will become a family heirloom. When wooden buttons weren't available in the size and small quantity that she required, her father came to the rescue, producing aromatic cedar buttons. By wearing her one hundred percent wool sweaters and wool socks, Lynda has been was able to turn down her furnace and conserve both energy and money.

I bought a sweater for my wife Donna after I'd finished shooting the story. I wasn't confident about choosing the right one, but Lynda told me that, if Donna didn't like the design or if it didn't fit, she'd find something else for her. I need not have worried; it fit really well and she loved the colour and design. In December of '94, Donna and I visited the 20th Anniversary One-of-a-Kind Canadian Craft Show. As we walked past the display booths, Donna recognized Lynda's sweater designs. After having a good chat with the designer, I ended up buying another beautiful sweater for my wife. This sweater was completely handknit, something this talented Canadian artist doesn't have time to do very often.

The Reid family dairy farm in Perth County near Stratford. David Reid is showing his two-year-old registered Holstein 'Dacrest Shasta' to his wife Jane and their sons Travis and Jackson.

DABOO FASHIONS

I received a phone call one morning from Virginia Kelly. Virginia had been an artist at Global and had taken early retirement to become a mother. She told me of a childhood friend who married a farmer, had children of her own, and now was not only designing clothes for her little ones, but she'd actually set up a business in her home. I drove out to the Reid farm, it's located on County Road 6, just southwest of Stratford. Although David Reid milks thirty Holsteins daily, it is by no means your typical Perth County dairy farm. It's become a fashion house, where fashion designer Jane Reid designs and makes her own line of children's clothes.

Jane and David bought the farm because Jane had great expectations of landing a job with the costume department at the Shakespearean Festival. It didn't happen; she wasn't hired. Jane is a graduate in fashion design from Oakville's Sheridan College. After leaving school she had her own ladies' wear shop; then she became a plant manager for an athletic clothing firm. Before she and David were married, Jane was a pattern maker for the now defunct Lady Manhattan . . . making blouses. "My interest in sewing started when I was making Barbie doll clothes out of Kleenex," said Jane. "The Kleenex kept ripping apart and I would get upset. My grandmother decided that she'd teach me how to sew. Then my mother taught me how to use patterns. Today, I've reached a stage were I can give them advice on sewing."

The daughter of a Brantford doctor named her clothing line Daboo after a childhood favourite, a stuffed Koala bear. "A lot of people driving by the farm see my sign at the end of the driveway, but are afraid to come in," she said. "They're worried that they might get stuck with me and feel obligated to buy something. I'm hoping that they won't feel that way, because it's a pretty relaxed atmosphere in here. Some people think that there won't be much to choose from, that I won't have much stock." Nothing could be farther from the truth. I couldn't believe my eyes when I went into the front section of the old farmhouse. Jane had more children's clothes on hand than most small stores. All on her own, she makes up to fifteen hundred outfits each year. That means that she must produce three to four garments every day. Jane loves her lifestyle choice and feels she's the luckiest person in the world. Not only can she stay at home and raise her two sons, Travis and Jackson, but she's also able to pursue a rewarding career. She admitted to me that she's had to make one concession though; she's hired a cleaning lady.

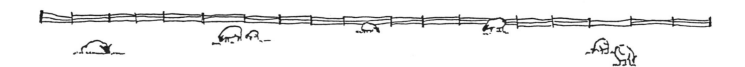

Jack Carson, the Windmill Man, with his apprentice John Hill and Jack's
dogs, Gypsy and Maggie.

THE WINDMILL MAN

When I was a lad growing up in rural Ontario, the working windmill was a common sight on almost every farm, pumping water for home and livestock. In the 1940s and early '50s hydro-electricity was brought into the farming communities and the majority of windmills gave way for electrically run water pumps. Thanks in part to Jack Carson, owner of the Priceville Windmill Company, those tall steel structures that were left to rust and fall apart in the fields are making a comeback. With the cost of electricity today, a lot of people are returning to the power of wind.

Jack's a former structural steelman who has admired windmills since he was a boy. "The windmill started as a hobby for me just over a dozen years ago," Jack said. "It's drawn a lot of attention from local and city people. With wind power being free, people are thinking in terms of using windmills to pump water in ponds and water to cattle."

Jack's right-hand man is his future son-in-law John Hill. When John's not working at the family farm, he's mastering the art of windmill restoration and maintenance from Jack.

Outside his country workshop, I shot scenes of the young apprentice soaring to the top of a windmill, standing in the bucket of a cherry-picker. To see what it actually looked like from that view, Jack lowered the bucket so that I could climb aboard with John. Fortunately, I've never been afraid of heights. High in the sky, John lifted the lid off the gearbox of a 1921 Chicago-made Aermotor. Then he gave it a checkup. The gears are all oil driven and must be checked and changed every six months. Lying alongside his workshop was an 1838 Aermotor, completely restored and painted white. On the fin in green lettering, were the owners' names, Steve and Caroline. It was ready to be trucked to a farm near Hillsburgh. Inside the workshop, Jack showed me an American-made Baker windmill designed with seventy-two retractable blades. It had been built in the early 1800s and still worked. Out front, Jack displays a variety of his products, including a Dempster, with a fourteen-foot head. The large windmill fan will lift water from a depth of six hundred feet below the surface of the ground. Not only are the windmills an efficient way to pump water, they're also part of our rural heritage.

John Durrant overhauling a turn-of-the-century Waltham pocket watch.

WATCHMAKER OF CREEMORE

John Durrant works at a profession that has almost become a lost art. He's a watchmaker and learned the trade from his late father Jim. His dad worked for a jeweller in Collingwood and, as a child of seven, John would sit near his father's workbench taking old clocks apart and putting them back together.

I visited John at The Clock Shoppe of Creemore in the fall of '94. After renting two locations in the village, he and his wife Nancy had just purchased the building next door on Mill Street. With living accommodations upstairs, the actual store will be three times larger than the cramped one when I did his story. Renovations were going on in his new building at that time. Even Nancy would have room to set up her business called Timeless Designs. She makes watch art jewellery from old clock and watch pieces.

It was literally like going back in time inside his tiny shop. Everywhere you looked, there were clocks. I had to be extremely careful manoeuvering around with my lights and tripod. John has clocks from Europe, some from the United States, and others made right here in Canada. There are clocks for sale and others are in to be repaired, like the 1790 mantel clock made by James Hanna of Quebec City. "It was once owned by Sir John Aird," said the watchmaker. "He was, from what we understand, the first president of the Canadian National Railway. Today, it's owned by his grandson and we're doing a restoration on it." There was a gorgeous American-made art nouveau which had been manufactured in Brooklyn, New York, around 1910.

Hunched over a workbench at the back of the shop was the watchmaker himself. Looking much like an old-world craftsman, John was overhauling a turn-of-the-century Waltham pocket watch. "Today there's no schooling that's per se in Canada where you can take a watchmaking course," said John. "There are a couple of night-school courses for clock repair but, as far as watchmaking goes, George Brown College in Toronto was the last one to offer it. From what I understand, the room is still full of tools and equipment, but not enough interest."

John, however, has taken on an apprentice. At the time of my story, Frank Gubbels was fifty years old. The former heavy-duty equipment mechanic spent years fixing graders and bulldozers. He's gone from monkey wrenches to tweezers and a magnifing glass. Frank travels over to Creemore from Barrie everyday to learn the craft. Belonging to a small, but tightly-knit network of fellow watch and clockmakers, John is able to locate parts for those old and rare clocks. If need be, he'll even create the necessary part.

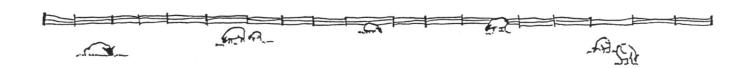

MINI REBIRTH

Culbert.

AUSTIN MINI REBIRTH

Global reporter John Darby lived in England for a number of years and worked as a television reporter with the British Broadcasting Corporation. We have chatted on many occasions about our love for certain things from abroad. During a long stint that John served on the assignment desk, he gave me a story that had come in on our news service about a senior citizen in Cambridge, Ontario, who was giving the tiny English Austin Mini another chance at life. John knew that I'd be interested in this one. As I drove along a county road on the outskirts of Cambridge, it wasn't hard to tell that I'd arrived at Bruce Rivers' property. It looked like an Austin Mini graveyard. It was hard to believe that all these broken-down relics were once the rage of Britain's swinging sixties.

Bruce Rivers is a jack of all trades with a background ranging from horticulture to metal fabricating. He was out by the garage putting the finishing touches on Shorty, a cut-down, two-seater Mini he'd created for his wife Rose. It was painted canary yellow and had been customized as a convertible. He showed me some of the other unusual vehicles that he'd made. What looked like a miniature cement truck was his pride and joy. "This is a ball mixer," he said. "Most people looking at it would think it was a cement mixer just as you did, Terry, but it's really a ball mixer. What's a ball mixer do? It mixes balls for bingo games or lotteries like the 649."

Two cast-off Minis and some spare parts from others made up a six-passenger, six-wheel limousine. His workmanship was incredible. You could not see the lines were one section was welded to another. The paint finish on all his vehicles were next to perfect.

His affection for this tiny English automobile was not the reason he began to customize the Austin; it was strictly economics. He told me that it would cost far too much to do the same thing to a full-size North American car.

Bruce remembers the exact day he began this unusual hobby. "It was May the 24th, 1987 at three thirty in the afternoon," he told me. "I know this, because I'd just finished putting the last stone on the house I was building for Rose and me." He and his wife have won several trophies over the years at Mini-Meet competitions held throughout Canada and the United States. Bruce claims that you can do anything you want if you put your mind to it.

Bruce Rivers passed away the week of February 13th, 1995. Those who knew this quiet, talented man will surely miss him.

DENTURE DOC

Finding this story was actually a story in itself. Every June, four of us get together for a Fathers' Day weekend in Beaver Valley at my brother-in-law Wayne Brennan's country place. It's located in the Owen Sound/Collingwood area. The weekend is a male-bonding thing that guys just have to do at least once a year. We have to be extra nice to our wives beforehand so that they'll let us go. We leave on a Friday evening and, to add to the fun, we take two of Wayne's vintage British sportscars with the convertible tops down. That's providing it's not raining, of course. Making up the foursome are our friends Doug McLellan and Ian Munroe.

About an hour from our Markham area homes, we stop for dinner at the Mono Cliff Inn. It's nestled in the hamlet of Mono Centre, just east of Orangeville. The four of us had just completed dinner that evening when Doug McLellan began talking to a young married couple sitting close by. Within minutes Doug called me over and introduced me to Ed and Krista Jurevicius. Ed's a denture therapist, a denture doc with a difference, because he does house calls. Ed is only one of a handful of denture therapists making house calls in this province. There's a great need for this specialized service geared towards seniors and invalids who can't get out to have their dentures relined or repaired. My friend Doug is also a tape editor in the Global newsroom and, when he discovered Ed's unique occupation, he knew this would make a good story.

I kept in touch with Ed over the next few months, waiting for him to find someone just right to be his patient and to be his co-star in my two-minute feature. In the late fall, Ed called. He'd found the right person. The man in need of denture work was Tom Parker, an eighty-five-year-old retired pharmaceutical salesman from Dublin, Ireland. He had recently moved to Canada to live with his son and daughter-in-law.

Tom has had his old dentures for over forty years and he's reached a point where he can neither bite nor chew. After removing the old dentures, Ed took an impression of Tom's mouth. Ed's soft-spoken, easy-going manner has got to be a plus for the job he's doing. Back at his Orangeville Clinic, Ed and his staff, including wife Krista, began to make a brand-new set of dentures for Tom. Ed, who graduated from Toronto's George Brown College, told me that it takes approximately two weeks to complete a full set. Ed's motto is We'll make you smile. With today's natural-looking dentures, that's no problem at all. "Once a person becomes used to them, the fears of looking different will soon fade," he said. "I highly recommend that dentures and mouth tissue be checked regularly." Ed claims that preventive dentistry is enabling people to keep their teeth longer. He feels that one day a full set of dentures will only be found in a museum.

Within two weeks, Ed was back with Tom's new set of dentures. This was a Kodak moment, as Ed slipped the new teeth into the big man's mouth. "Open, close your teeth together . . . Perfect. Give me smile . . . Bigger smile . . . Good," said Ed. And what did Tom look like? Well, I had witnessed the before and after with my own eyes and this new set looked as if he'd been born with them. Tom Parker, the Dubliner, looked marvellous.

Louie Fotia and Patricia Coates visiting Frank Serratore in his south
London shoe repair shop.

FRANK'S SHOE REPAIR

How often can you get something for nothing without a string attached? Well, at Frank Serratore's Shoe Repair in south London, you can get free peanuts, licorice, coffee and even free laughs just by walking in the door. You don't even have to bring your shoes in to be mended. Frank has a toy parrot named Polly hanging from a hook and, when a child comes in, Frank's pet bird talks. People love to visit the proud Italian; he's a quality craftsman, and he's a friend to hundreds of Londoners.

I couldn't believe my eyes when I entered his tiny, crowded shop. Every square inch of wall space was covered with photographs and memorabilia. He's a sports nut. When it comes to hockey, it's the Montreal Canadiens, and his baseball team is the New York Yankees. If you look closely you'll spot a picture of his son Joe with Wayne Gretzky. Another photograph shows both sons, Joe and Vince.

Born in London, Ontario, Frank has been working with shoes since 1932. He started helping his father Giuseppe at the age of eight. He polished shoes and delivered repaired ones on his bicycle. By 1945 Frank had his own store in east London. Eventually he moved downtown to Wellington Street. In 1987, after thirty-six years in the city centre, he relocated his business to Commissioners Road.

Music has always played a big part in his life. During World War II, Frank was a member of the Royal Canadian Artillery Band. An accomplished clarinet and saxophone player, he has played with London's biggest dance bands. He was with the Lionel Thornton Band for twenty-seven years, making Guy Lombardo-style music. He was with Phil Murphy, Bubs Jamison, Hoppy Hopkins, and the Len Langley Band and fifteen years with the New Modernaires. Directed by Ron Shadbolt, the fifteen-piece orchestra had a Glenn Miller sound. "There was the Martin Bounty Band," he said, "one of the best directors you ever want to play with." He still plays every Wednesday night with The Moonliters at the Highland Country Club. "A lot of these people are retired," said Frank, "but they want to keep their music up." Many of his musician friends pop in just to chat.

While I was there, one of his favourite customers brought a pair of boots in. Patricia Coates is a Dublin-born singer/actress, who gets a kick out of Frank's Italian charm.

"Sweetheart, how are ya?" said Frank.

"Ah, go on you old charmer ya," Patricia replied.

"So what's the problem with your boots?" said he.

"I just need a heel on the back."

"I've got to level all this up and recap it so you'll be able to do your dancing like you always do."

"I won't be wearing them dancing."

"You won't?" said he.

"Will they be ready by the fifteenth, before I go back to Ireland for Christmas?"

"I'll have them ready anytime you want," Frank said.

Another visitor that morning was Louie Fotia, a young cousin. Louie's a local hairdresser and captain of London City in the Canadian National Soccer League. While I was shooting scenes of Frank working, Louie suggested a protein product to strengthen Patricia's hair. I thought Patricia's hair looked healthy just the way it was.

Frank told me that he'd been married to Rose for forty-eight years. When I asked him about retirement, he said he has no plans; he's having too much fun fixing shoes and entertaining his friends.

Photograph: John Wiggins

Signcrafter Shane Durnford at work in Creemore's
one-time casket factory.

HAND-CARVED SIGNS

A few years ago I was in Creemore doing a story on artist Stephanie Stearn. At that time she ran a gallery on Mill Street called Vanquish, an art gallery for "yet to be famous artists." When I'd finished my story Stephanie suggested that we visit a signmaker across the road.

Shane Durnford calls himself a signcrafter. His studio is housed in the village's one-time casket factory. The one hundred and twenty-five-year-old building is owned by the brewery next door, one of the best micro-breweries in the land. Years ago, before I started doing my own stories, fellow beer enthusiast and friend Paul Dalby and I did a feature on Creemore Springs Brewery Limited. It was John Wiggins, the owner of the brewery and a designer himself, who talked Shane into setting up his sign shop. Shane's philosophy is that signs on businesses and old houses should look as if they belong. And wherever you look in this pretty village, you'll see his handsome hand-carved signs. There's one hanging from the front of the Sovereign Restaurant and another on the Fawcett Funeral Home. Even St. Luke's Anglican Church has a Durnford sign.

Shane is basically self-taught, although he did complete a sign course at Toronto's George Brown College. He works completely by hand, using his own designs. With years of study and experimentation, his carved signs look much like the ones that the craftsmen of the 1700s did in England and Europe. "In Canada, most of the sign business is commercial," said Shane. "It's get it in and get it out. With me, it's more of a lifestyle. I want to make a living at it, but I want to make the kind of signs that I like to make. People appreciate quality and appreciate what you can do for them. Customers are more discriminating these days. They're tired of plastic and mass-produced articles."

Shane's wife, Jackie, looks after marketing, promotion and workload scheduling. Her husband gives her credit for a lot of their sign concepts. "With all my projects," he said, "I try to design them to suit the personality of the people who commissioned me, their home and its architecture. I use colours of the landscape, the shape of the hills, and the surrounding area." Personal consultation is a very important part of the process. He ensures that the size, design, colour, and detail reflect each individual client and their property. The Durnfords also guarantee their work for five years. Shane feels he owes the success of his business to people's general return to appreciation of quality.

Throughout Grey-Bruce Counties, Ed Barclay is known as "Mr. Meccano."

MECCANO

Joe Hodgins and I grew up together in Lucan. He lived on a farm on the outskirts of the village and during the early '50s, he could tell you more about the moon, the stars, and the galaxy then anyone I knew, including most adults. Joe had something that I'd never seen before. It was called a Meccano Set, the first construction toy of its kind. The 1901 British invention was originally named "mechanics made easy." Meccano is a miniature construction system of metal strips and plates punched with small holes. With a small screwdriver, wrench, nuts and bolts, a child engineer can create wonderful structures. The sets came with gears, rods, and cranks. The child's parents could even buy them an electric motor.

In January of 1990, I did my first story as a cameraman/reporter for Global. The subject I chose was Meccano. I drove to Owen Sound where I had set up an appointment with "Canada's Meccano Man," Ed Barclay. When I did the story with him, it was thought that he had the largest collection of Meccano in Canada, approximately two tons, in his basement. When I arrived, Ed met me at the door with his two little daughters, and took me off to see the collection.

"Well I guess I got my first Meccano set in 1945," Ed said. "My father bought it for me immediately after the war ended. The thing I remember most, especially when I was sick, my dad would make a model for me. When I'd wake up in the morning, it would be on the bedside table for me to play with. You can't give a child a Meccano set and expect him to build little models by themselves unaided. There has to be parental intervention with it. Guidance, show them what to do. How to use the tools and how to build the models. How to read the instruction books. Once you've shown the child how to work the Meccano set, they'll get a hold of it and do it themselves."

Ed claims that Meccano is an indoor hobby and can't be spoiled by snow or rain. More than that, it keeps the mind active. Ed told me that it's certainly not just for children. It's also a great form of therapy for seniors unable to get out and about. Ed is also the editor of the *Canadian Meccanoman's Newsletter*. It's a small-run magazine of facts, stories, and plans for model builders and collectors.

In October of '94, I phoned Ed to to tell him of this book and that I wanted to use his story. I told him that I was going to be in the Owen Sound area and asked if I could drop by and take his picture. When I arrived, almost five years after doing my story on him, I was met by Ed and one of his daughters. Ed looked exactly the same, but I said to his daughter, "Wow, have you grown." "Actually Terry, this is our latest addition," said Ed, "she wasn't even born when you were here last." As we chatted, I took his photograph. He's more involved in Meccano now than ever before. His newsletter has been renamed *Canadian Meccano News* and is a smart glossy covered quarterly that subscribers receive by airmail. Ed is also known throughout the Grey-Bruce school system as Mr. Meccano. He travels around with his Mobile Creativity Unit giving short sessions to students seven to twelve years of age. He talks and demonstrates such topics as pulleys and levers. Ed also organizes an annual Meccano Extravaganza in Owen Sound with exhibitors coming from as far away as New York, California, Quebec and Saskatchewan.

By the way, Meccano ceased operations in Liverpool, England in 1978, after seventy-seven years. New owners resurrected the company in Calais, France in 1983.

PLAYING CARD COLLECTOR

When it comes to playing cards, I don't. As a child I played fish. I watched my father and uncles play cribbage, and periodically I'd watch the grade thirteen students play cards at the back of our school bus enroute to Medway High School in Arva. So I guess, with my lack of interest, I was surprised when Global news editor Tom Boldt suggested I talk to entertainment reporter Elaine Loring. Her father-in-law was mad about playing cards and had thousands of decks in his collection.

Ben Bornstein doesn't play anymore, he just collects. He loves to study the history behind each deck and admire the artistic way that each one was produced. The North York man began his collection in 1972 and is a founding member of the American Antique Deck Collectors Club. He has more than two thousand packs representing over sixty countries stored neatly in special plastic boxes on his custom-built shelves.

Two of the decks caught my attention when I was shooting the story. Goodall's Victorian playing cards were manufactured in England in 1897. The gilt-edged, round-cornered deck was produced to celebrate Queen Victoria's reign on the throne. In 1915, Goodall's put out a pack called City of Toronto. Each card had a different photograph of Toronto, including one from the harbour showing the city's skyline before the Royal York Hotel was built. Another one was produced in the United States in 1896, titled The Stage. Each card bore four different photographs of famous people of the American stage. Ben has acquired cards made for the past eight presidents of the United States of America. He has cards in every imaginable shape and size, square, round, triangular, concave, convex, and S-shaped. They range from one-quarter inch to one foot in size.

Ben told me that playing cards have been around for six centuries. At one time they were banned in Britain, thought to be the work of the devil. Prisoners of war made cards of bone. Cards were written on and used as currency, as invitations, and as death notices. Many famous artists over the years have designed cards. Salvador Dali designed a deck that was produced in France by Puiforcat in 1967, and Ben has one of his. He has cards promoting and condemning cigarettes. There are cards for ocean liners, railways, and airlines.

Ben showed me a pack made in the U.S.S.R. "This deck was made in 1967 to celebrate the 150th year of the playing card industry in Russia," he said. "Most collectors will try to have one of these packs in their collection. This is an aluminum deck made for the Pan-Am Exposition of 1901. It is quite scarce. If a card gets bent, you can never straighten it out properly again."

Today the retired automotive parts salesman keeps himself busy cataloguing his cards and corresponding with collectors all over the world. His wife Jean has always been extremely supportive; her favourite deck is from Japan. It's called Okeeowee and comes in a pretty velvet box with a different Japanese dancer on each card.

I ended my story by putting myself on camera. I held up an old playing card and looking straight into the lens. I said: "I can't show you this hand-painted card that was made in France during the 1820s, because if I held it to a bright light you'd be able to see a pornographic picture. I'm Terry Culbert for Global News in North York, Ontario."

On January 11, 1995, Ben became a grandfather again. His daughter-in-law Elaine Loring gave birth to a son, Max Loring Bornstein.

FISHING REEL COLLECTOR

It's not uncommon to find Gerry Grimminck and his son Jerry casting their lines into Sharon Creek, near Delaware, just west of London. Gerry has been fishing since he was a young boy in his native Holland and, when he was six, his grandfather gave him his first fishing rod, a sixteen-foot, one-piece bamboo pole. A few years ago, this avid fisherman began collecting rods and reels and today he's probably got the largest collection in Ontario, if not Canada. In his spare time he'll search out flea markets and garage sales all across North America. Sometimes he'll buy a whole tackle box to get one reel. His collection, which has pieces dating back to the 1800s, consists of over five hundred rods and more than six hundred reels. In the basement of his Delaware home, Gerry has a good deal of it on display. He's even made special cases to carry them in when he gives talks at local fishing clubs. He does this for free.

Gerry has a Julius Vom Hofe reel patented in October 1889. His Winchester 4250 reel was manufactured in the United States at the turn of this century. His Meisselbach tripart fishing reel was made in 1920. His "Hurd Super-caster" was manufactured in Detroit, Michigan, and it came complete with a three-foot, six-inch steel rod. He told me that during World War II, there was a void in fishing history. It seems that everything went for the war effort. It was during this period that fibreglass was invented and the fibreglass fishing rod was released on the retail market. It's easy to tell an early fibreglass rod because they were clear. Coloured fibreglass came a few years later.

Gerry made a special trip to Winnipeg, Manitoba, to visit a hardware store that was going out of business. He got himself thirty-eight old reels that were brand new. As a matter of fact, they were all in their original cartons. He hasn't put a dollar figure on his collection because he doesn't sell any of it. His rod collection ranges from solid bamboo to old split cane, from steel to fibreglass. He's recorded all the data about his rod and reel collection in a computer.

Gerry's dream is to start a fishing museum. He'd incorporate his collection, along with old lures and antique outboard motors from other collectors. His dream springs from his discovery of a fishing museum in Hayward, Wisconsin. He'd make his museum non-profit with no government involvement. It would be wheelchair accessible and Gerry would have it run by fishing enthusiasts. Good luck to you, Gerry.

Photograph: Michael Hanley, The Spectator

Gary Duschl is in the 1995 Guinness Book of Records because his gum-wrapper chain is the longest in the world. It measures 12, 105 feet in length.

GUM WRAPPER CHAMP

Gary Duschel is in *The Guinness Book of Records 1995*. The Waterdown man has collected enough gum wrappers to form a chain measuring 12,105 feet in length. That makes his chain almost a mile longer than the existing record set by Kathy Ushler of Redmond, Washington. It all began for Gary as a fad back in 1965, you know, the type of thing that only a fourteen-year-old high school student might do. Gary was attending Waterdown District High School and word spread throughout the classrooms that some kid was collecting gum wrappers. Before long he had fellow students supplying him with wrappers.

Gary's wrappers aren't just from any brand, as I had envisioned. No, sir, they're from one manufacturer only . . . Wrigley's. And he collects only three flavours, Doublemint, Spearmint, and Juicyfruit. I had pictured them being Scotch-taped together. Well, I was wrong on that count too, because he carefully folds and links each individual wrapper onto the tail of the chain. No tape or glue is used whatsoever. Gary's award-winning chain consists of half a million gum wrappers. "What I do is fold the wrappers into individual links," said Gary, "then I add these links, one at a time, to the chain. Each of the links adds a quarter of an inch to the length of the chain."

At Wrigley Headquarters Canada, in the heart of Don Mills, I asked product manager Andy Alderman what Wrigley thought of all this. "When you think of it, it's pretty impressive," said Andy. "He's taken all these wrappers and pieced them together to form a gum-wrapper chain that would span the length of sixty-one hockey arenas. I'd say he was an outstanding customer."

Gary keeps his treasure in three specially designed glass cases in the den of his home. Sometimes, he'll string the chain through the house, over door frames, along the top of pictures on the wall, across the kitchen refrigerator and into the family room, so he can sit and watch television with his wife Debbie. I asked Gary if there was anything he'd like to say about this unusual hobby.

"I'd like to thank all the wonderful people that have saved me wrappers all these years," he said. "I'd like to give a special thanks to my wife Debra for being so tolerant with me all this time." I'd second that last statement. Congratulations Gary, as the new record holder of the world's longest gum-wrapper chain and thanks for sending me my own autographed copy of *The Guinness Book of Records 1995*.

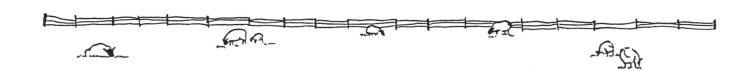

CANADIAN PIG MUSEUM

Philip King is a copy and layout editor for the sports department of Canada's National Newspaper, the *Globe and Mail.* There's another side to this young newspaper man; he's got a passion for the cloven-hoofed mammal known as the pig. As a matter of fact, Philip is hog wild about swine and is curator of his very own in-home museum devoted entirely to "pigobilia." He's even registered the name, Canadian Pig Museum.

At his parents' farmhouse just north of Bolton, he's amassed more than three thousand pig-related items. Fortunately I carry a wide-angle adapter for my lens, because the room wasn't much bigger than a shoebox. There are pig books, photos, and key-chains. There are stuffed toy pigs, puzzles, and salt and pepper shakers. He has a pig mask that he wears on special occasions and cartoons of curly-tailed critters on bumper stickers.

How did he get interested in this hobby? "I was working on a pig farm while attending university," he said, "and one day when I was looking after the pigs, I found a little one that was extremely sick. I brought it home and made a valiant effort to save its life. I bottle fed it, but it died that same night. Since that time I've devoted my life to pigs."

Philip's massive collection all began from a tiny porcelain Red Rose Tea giveaway of a pig that his sister gave him. Then friends began keeping an eye out for him. A colleague from the *Globe and Mail* found a pig artifact in Europe. He travelled through six countries with it and, each time he entered customs, the parcel showed up looking like a bomb. He apparently had one heck of a job explaining at each airport what it was and why he was bringing it back to Canada.

For the past decade Philip has made an earnest effort to advance the knowledge of pigs, pig lore, and Canada's pork industry. His goal is to protect and enhance the development and appreciation of the pig in Canada. After spending a couple of hours at the Canadian Pig Museum, I learned that pigs have been domesticated since the year 7,000 B.C., that some of the world's best pork is produced in Israel, that Ontario's Perth County raises 600,000 pigs annually, and Porky Pig was born on the backlot of Hollywood's Warner Brothers Studios in 1937.

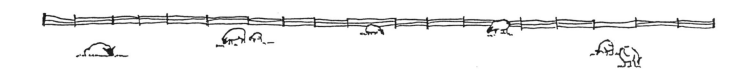

Photographer Thomas Connon (self-portrait)

Photograph: John Connon

Young men in the Gorge. Hats tossed in the air were actually pinned to the rock surface.

CONNON PHOTOGRAPHY

I have made my entire career in photography, purchasing my first still camera when I was sixteen years old. It was a Yashica-C twin-lens reflex and I used it to take pictures as a teenager for the *Exeter Times-Advocate* and the *London Free Press*. In 1967, I bought my first 35 mm camera, then in my mid-30s I upgraded and purchased a 35 mm with a built-in light meter. At this point, I thought I'd died and gone to heaven. The walls of my home and the Feathers Pub in Toronto are filled with photographs that I've taken over the years using my two 35 mms. But it wasn't until I was in my early fifties that I learned that a father and son, living in the Wellington County village of Elora, were not only brilliant photographers but were inventors as well.

This is the story of Thomas and John Connon. Thomas Connon was born in the Parish of Udney, Aberdeenshire, Scotland on the 14th day of September 1832. As Thomas grew into manhood, he apprenticed in the wholesale grocery business in the city of Aberdeen. He had always been interested in drawing and painting. When the first signs of this new invention called photography appeared, he was hooked. He read anything and everything that was written on the subject. The *Art Journal,* a British monthly periodical, featured stories on the latest photographic developments. These were featured at the Great Exhibition of 1851, held at the Crystal Palace in London.

At the age of twenty he became restless and emigrated to Canada. Thomas spent his first winter in Beamsville on the Niagara pennisula and moved to Elora in March of 1853. While working for James Philip, a local general merchant, Thomas met and married Jean Keith, daughter to John and Mrs. Keith. The Keiths were early settlers to the Elora area, arriving there in 1834.

During their first year of marriage, Thomas commenced his experiments with photography. Over the next few years the couple opened their own store with photography as a sideline. In 1861, Thomas wrote to his aunt in Aberdeen reporting that he was still making them pictures and that he had a place fitted up behind the store and that he would call Jean, his wife, to attend the shop when anyone wanted pictures taken. Two years later he had expanded his work beyond standard portraits and wrote his aunt in Scotland to say: "I am making outside pictures instantaneous, one showing the wave of the swollen river, another of a cattle fair, the moving objects in each being quite distinct."

The officers of the Elora Rifle Company (1866)

Photograph: Thomas Connon

The Elora Gorge in the late 1800s

By 1874, his son John, now twelve, began to follow in his father's footsteps. John was given a corner in the darkroom with his own developing material. He was also given the use of his father's stereoscopic camera from the time he was old enough to carry it. The two developed a lively relationship as photographers, which resulted in the pair coming up with several photographic inventions. Connon senior developed a gelatine roll film holder in 1881, an improvement on the gelatine dry-plate glass negatives introduced to the mass market at the end of the 1870s. But, alas, Thomas never patented it. The patent was later secured by the Eastman Kodak Company of Rochester, New York. Kodak went onto revolutionize the photographic business, making fast and easy-loading cameras available to the masses. A year later, son John invented a shutter for the lens. John saw that the proper place for a shutter was at the small opening of the diaphram between the lenses. With the use of a rubber bulb attached to the shutter by an umbilical cord, the photographer could open and close the shutter at will, allowing for adjustable exposure times. It was patented by John in the United States.

The most important invention in John Connon's career was the whole-circle panoramic camera. According to a *London Free Press* article of 1924, this was the first panoramic camera ever built. It was patented in the United States in 1890. This camera came about as the result of John's desire to take a picture of Elora, showing its remarkable beauty in its entirety. After the patent went through, John took a position with a photographic supply firm in New York City, in an attempt to promote what was being called the new wonder camera. During his two-year stay, John took a number of unique photographs of New York City, including its harbour and streets. When he felt that he'd spent enough time and money on the development of the panoramic camera, he returned to Elora to once again work with his father.

John began specializing in exterior shots, doing his portrait and group photographs amongst the rocks of the Elora Gorge. His father Thomas, who by then was in failing health, continued to do work in their studio. Thomas Connon died in 1899. J. M. Shaw, editor of the *Elora Express* wrote as follows: "The writer first met Mr. Connon in 1859. He was one of the foremost men of the rising village and took an active part in everything pertaining to the welfare of its inhabitants. His artistic eye saw so many new and ever recurring beauties about Elora."

John, with the help of his mother, carried on the family business after the death of his father. According to a *London Free Press* article of 1924, the mother was a woman of unusual intelligence and refinement. She was ever a joy and an inspiration to her son John and to all who knew her.

Jean Connon never lost faith in the inventions of her husband and son, and often offered suggestions which solved a number of problems.

We have a lot to thank the Connons for. These early pioneers of photography were partially responsible for the simplicity of taking pictures today. Elora resident Bob Reynolds was a great help for me when I was putting this story together for television and for this book. Bob and his dear wife Angie are tireless volunteers for an annual event in that village called "In love with Elora Month." When I was doing my television story, Bob was my interview. He sat amongst some of the camera equipment the Connons had invented and used.

Just as a footnote to this story, Elora is the most sketched, painted, and photographed village in all of Ontario. During "In love with Elora Month," merchants' windows display art and photographs, and on the eastern edge of the village, the Wellington County Museum has become the centrepiece for the month-long event. I had set up two stories at that time in Elora, one about the artists with museum director/curator Ellen Langlands, and the other with Bob Reynolds on the Connons. We were all getting together the morning I arrived to iron out the logistics. When Bob and I looked at each other, we knew that we'd met before. It turned out that we'd been neighbours in Scarborough a few years before. Bob and Angie had moved to the quieter lifestyle of Elora and they love it.

From the collection of the Wellington County Museum and Archives

Panoramic print showing view of Elora, Ontario in winter time taken from south side of Grand River, east of Elora: following prominent buildings are identified left to right: Knox Presbyterian Church, St. Mary's Roman Catholic Church, Elora Public School, Elora Carpet Factory, stone mill at Aboyne

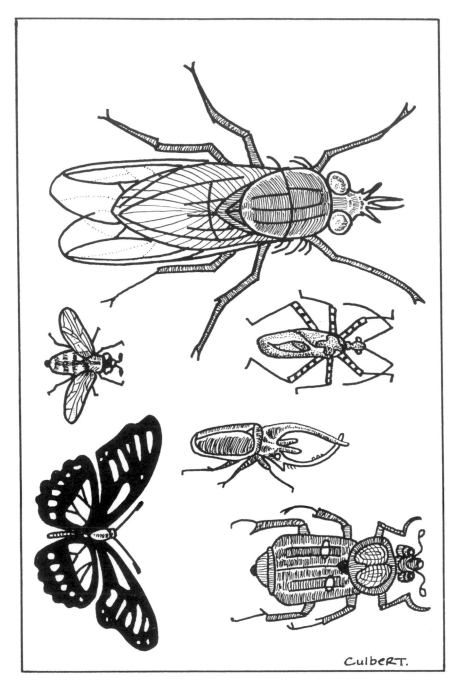

CulbeRT.

INSECT COLLECTION

I arrived at the University of Guelph to do a feature on the oldest insect collection in Canada. It predates Confederation by four years. The collection is housed at the Ontario Agricultural College, in the Department of Environmental Biology.

I met graduate student and part-time curator Ian Smith and he began showing me the facilities. A few minutes later, the door opened and in walked a moustached man who resembled the Hollywood actor Richard Chamberlain. Dr. Stephen Marshall is an insect systematist, a person who specializes in bugs. We greeted each other, then it was off to see the bugs. These little creatures are housed in huge cabinets that move electrically. To look at a particular species, a push of a button separates the cabinets, opening up an aisle for you to enter. There's row upon row of locker-style doors. Behind each door are twenty-four glass-topped drawers. When you pull out the appropriate drawer you find each individual insect labelled as to where, when, and by whom it was caught, and the scientific name of the insect. *Nicophorus Americanus*, that's the American Burying Beetle; *Leptoglossus* is the Western Conifer Seed Bug.

With my superb lens, I was able to fill the frame with the tips of Dr. Marshall's fingers as he held a pin to which a *Polystoechotes Punctatus* was attached. "This is a Giant Lace-wing," he said. "It used to be quite common in Ontario. Many of these specimens are from the Guelph area, all collected prior to 1950. There are no specimens of this species from Eastern North America after 1950, and we don't know why."

Dr. Marshall picked up another pin. Mounted on it, and extremely hard to see with the naked eye, was a *Poecilographa*

Decora. "This little polka-dotted beauty is probably a Snail Killing Fly. It's actually a mystery. We think it feeds on snails because that's what its relatives do. Its biology is unknown and I find that mystery really fascinating," he said.

"This collection is essential for insect identification; it's essential for basic research and biodiversity. It documents changes in insect ranges. Where else are you going to look to find out what insects were in Southern Ontario fifty years ago, except in this collection? Where else are you going to look to find out what wasn't in Southern Ontario fifty years ago, except this collection?" Dr. Marshall compares his insect collection to a library. Every individual speciman is like an irreplaceable book. I think that's a pretty darn good analogy. The day I visited, Xuekui Sun, a Ph.D. student from China, was examining a parasitic fly.

The Guelph collection is the oldest in Canada and the second oldest in North America. With over one million species, it's not the biggest. One of the largest on the continent is with Agriculture Canada in Ottawa, where they've collected over fifteen million specimens since 1886. It's a big job to protect and keep the collection in orderbut it's done by a combination of part-time and volunteer students.

Ian Smith and Dr. Marshall co-wrote a paper after they analyzed thirty closely related fly species. Many of them are new to science, including one that was collected from the shores of Meech Lake. What did they name this newly discovered fly? *Mulroneyi,* of course. They sent a note to Prime Minister Brian Mulroney telling him of their discovery and its name. He wasn't amused.

KENTE PORTAGE

Michael Fitzgerald is the head writer in our newsroom and a man in love with Prince Edward County. He and his wife Janet spend almost every summer holiday in this magnificent area of Eastern Ontario. In the fall of '91, Michael asked me if I'd ever heard of Fort Kente or the Kente Portage. When I told him I hadn't, he suggested it might make a good story.

For centuries, natives portaged across the narrow section of land separating the Bay of Quinte from Lake Ontario. When the explorer Champlain passed through that area in 1615, it was already a beaten path. The slightly irregular route, a mile and a half in length, is known as the Kente Portage. It's the oldest continuously used road in Ontario. It forms the county line between Northumberland County to the north and Prince Edward County to the south. It crosses Highway 33 at Carrying Place. In 1800, Carrying Place was a veritable metropolis in the wilderness.

Three heritage homes still remain on the portage: there's the home of Colonel Robert Charles Wilkins, a military man; in 1810, Asa Weller built his red-brick house as a stagecoach-way station and tap house; Captain Robert Young, a close friend of Lieutenant Governor John Graves Simcoe, erected a house for himself along this road. Captain Young was a United Empire Loyalist who first settled in Nova Scotia before moving west. The Kente Portage comes to an end at Wellers Bay, which eventually joins the open waters of Lake Ontario. When the War of 1812 broke out between the Americans and the British, the Americans had already gained control of the north shore of Lake Ontario so it was extremely important to protect this vital area. In 1813, the British built Fort Kente on the shores of Wellers Bay. It was manned by the Provincial Dragoons.

The small blockhouse ensured safe passage for soldiers and merchants alike.

The celebration of this long-neglected historical route and the rebuilding of Fort Kente are all thanks to the efforts of Dr. Paul Germain, President of the Kente Portage Heritage Conservation Society. Under his direction, an exact replica of the original fort is being constructed, twenty feet square by thirty feet in height. The Society has had absolutely no government funding for the project. Private companies, individuals, and clubs have donated money and many have volunteered their labour. The day I was there, a group of men representing Branch 110 of the Royal Canadian Legion in Trenton dropped off a five thousand dollar cheque towards building expenses.

Dr. Germain and his wife Edythe live on the Kente Portage. They purchased the old Weller House in 1987. Edythe is an artist and has set up a gallery in the front room, probably the same room where soldiers and villagers drank their beer from pewter tankards, nearly two hundred years ago. The Germains moved here from Montreal where Paul had been a Doctor of Philosophy, teaching at the University of Montreal, Concordia, and the University of Quebec. I asked him why he, a francophone, knowing that there had been two French forts in the same area before the British built Fort Kente, hadn't built a French fort? "We had less information about the French forts," said Paul, "they were built before 1720."

I have a wonderful job and believe me I know it. I travel across Ontario meeting the best people and seeing the greatest sights. I'd passed through Carrying Place a few times, but I had no idea of its fascinating history until my colleague Michael Fitzgerald told me about the Kente Portage.

Major William Avery (Billy) Bishop of the Royal Flying Corps. At the age of twenty-four, he had won the Victoria Cross, the Distinguished Service Order and Bar, and Military Cross. (October 1917).

BILLY BISHOP MUSEUM

During World War II, my uncle Ivan Culbert went overseas with the Royal Canadian Regiment. Uncle Ivan's brothers Ken and Mel joined the Royal Canadian Air Force, Uncle Ken with Transport Command, transporting VIPs and secret documents across the Atlantic. My father, Mel, remained in Canada. He was a radar technician who suffered nosebleeds everytime he flew. Eventually he was posted to Toronto as a draftsman in the RCAF's Works Department. After the war, their younger brother, my uncle Mert, joined the Royal Canadian Navy. Because of the involvement that my family had with the military in my early life, I have always had a lot of respect for the men and women who served and those that died for our freedom.

When I heard about the Billy Bishop Museum in Owen Sound, it became a must on my story agenda. In the fall of '94, I did a story for the *News at Noon* which ran on Remembrance Day, November the 11th.

Earlier that week, I drove up to Owen Sound to meet with Group Captain A. J. Bauer, founder and chairman of Billy Bishop Heritage. The native of Desboro, which is just south of Owen Sound, had served thirty-five years with the Royal Canadian Air Force. He'd been a flying instructor, then a fighter pilot in Europe assigned to NATO. We'd decided to meet and have lunch at the Tein-Bo Chinese restaurant before shooting the story. When I arrived, I met the group captain and student volunteer Steve Dieter. The Wilfrid Laurier University history major worked at the museum as a historian and public relations man. Even while attending Owen Sound Collegiate, Steve had been a history buff.

He went on to tell me of some of the famous people who had gone to his high school. He mentioned Dr. Norman Bethune and Agnes Macphail, the first woman elected to

Canada's Parliament in 1921. There was of course Billy Bishop and then a man my wife Donna and I wake up to each morning, CHFI Radio's Don Danard. "Something else that's not well known," he said, "was that, in Owen Sound's Greenwood Cemetery, there are buried three military men who all received the Victoria Cross. They were Sergeant Tommy Holmes and Air Marshall Billy Bishop of the First World War, and Lieutenant Colonel David Currie of World War Two."

William Avery Bishop was born the 8th of February 1894, in a huge brick home that his parents had built. The house, located at 948 3rd Avenue West, was purchased from the Bishop family in 1987 and turned into the Billy Bishop Museum.

Billy's mother was Margaret Louise Greene and his father William Avery Bishop the First. Will, as he was called, was a lawyer and registrar of Grey County. Billy had an older brother, Worth, born ten years before him. A second brother died at the early age of seven and a sister Louie was born a year after Billy.

At the age of seventeen, Billy left home for the Royal Military College in Kingston. His years at RMC were not great. There were many who figured young Billy Bishop would not amount to much, he was well known for his spirited high jinks and on two occasions he stepped over the line. His first incident involved stealing a canoe, drinking alcohol, and being absent without leave. The second serious matter arose when he cheated on a final exam. He left the college in disgrace.

It so happened that World War One had just begun. Billy, now twenty years old, enlisted with the Mississauga Horse, a Toronto unit. Soon after, he transferred to the 7th Canadian Mounted Rifles stationed in London, Ontario.

122

The young lieutenant excelled in military life, displaying leadership qualities that were recognized by his superiors. He became a machine-gun unit instructor, then headed the riding class. In February of 1915, he became engaged to Margaret Burden, a granddaughter of Timothy Eaton, the founder of Eaton's department stores. She would become his inspiration throughout the war in Europe.

Once overseas, Billy didn't remain with the cavalry for long. He traded in his horse to join the Royal Flying Corps. In the beginning he had to serve time as a professional air observer. Eager to be a pilot, he began training in October of 1916 and, by March of the following year, he'd received orders to report to Fighter Squadron Number 60 at Izel les Hameaux in France.

During his first six weeks of combat, Billy's record for destroying enemy aircraft was remarkable. In addition to his stamina, he possessed superior eyesight, enabling him to spot enemy targets off in the distance. By the end of June 1917, Billy Bishop's count stood at thirty-one.

Before the war ended in 1918, Billy had destroyed seventy-two enemy aircraft, making him the foremost British Empire pilot of World War One.

At the age of twenty-four, he'd won the Victoria Cross, the Distinguished Service Order, and the Military Cross. He became a household name throughout Britain, Canada, and the United States. Billy was sent home to undertake a speaking tour. Close to six thousand people were waiting for the hometown hero as his train arrived at the Owen Sound station. While back in Canada, he married Margaret at the Timothy Eaton Memorial Church in Toronto.

Returning overseas, he was given command of a new fighter squadron, Number 85, the Flying Foxes. In May of 1918 the squadron flew to France. Within four weeks, he'd personally destroyed another twenty-five enemy aircraft. He was awarded the Distinguished Flying Cross.

When the war ended later that year, over half a million service personnel returned to Canada, including the famous Canadian hero.

With fellow Canadian airman and Victoria Cross recipient William George Barker, he established the Bishop-Barker Aeroplanes Limited. They provided passenger service between Toronto and the vacation area of Muskoka. The company went bankrupt two years later. Billy and Margaret decided to move to England where Billy was offered a position selling the foreign rights to a new method of producing iron pipe. The years between 1925 and 29 were very successful but in October of 1929, the stock market crashed and the Bishops, ruined, returned to Canada. Billy became vice-president of sales with McColl-Frontenac Oil in Montreal.

In 1938, Billy was made an Honorary Air Marshall of the Royal Canadian Air Force. With the outbreak of World War Two the next year, he became Director of Recruiting for the RCAF During the war he became more than a recruiter, he became a morale booster in both Canada and the United Kingdom. As an Air Marshall he was having his uniforms tailored, as we discovered when I was shooting the story, by Anderson and Sheppard of London's famous Savile Row.

In 1952, Billy Bishop retired to Palm Beach, Florida. In 1956 he died peacefully in his sleep. His body was cremated and his ashes were laid in the family plot in Owen Sound's Greenwood Cemetery. At the time of his death, he was survived by his wife Margaret, a son Arthur, a daughter Marise, his sister Louise, and his brother, Colonel Worth Bishop.

The Culbert brothers of Lucan, Ontario, received a pen and pencil set from the Township of Biddulph. Every man and woman from Biddulph who volunteered to serve in the Canadian military during World War II received this gift at the end of the war. Left to right: Uncle Ken (Flight Lieutenant/RCAF), Uncle Ivan (Sergeant/RCR), and my father Mel (Sergeant/RCAF).

Photograph courtesy of Ron Laidlaw/The London Free Press

The Billy Bishop Heritage is an incorporated group of dedicated volunteers interested in maintaining and preserving the memory of one of Canada's greatest air aces. The Heritage, under the direction of Group Captain A. J. Bauer, financially support the Billy Bishop Museum. As I was driving east out of Owen Sound, I couldn't help but notice their municipal airport; it bore the name of the famous airman.

Photograph courtesy of Doug McLellan

Curator Jim Jones with volunteers Nettie Wallman, Colleen Belanger, and
Maureen Hotts, in the Bunker.

THE BUNKER

Jim Jones went back to England, the land of his birth, during World War II as a member of the Signal Corps with the Canadian Army. When the war ended in 1945, Jim returned to the town of Cobalt bringing a few mementos of the war. He went back to the job he'd been trained for—mining.

All the time he spent underground digging for silver, he thought of how to add to his military collection. "I came home with a few little articles and just kept adding to it, and now I'm addicted. I don't regret a minute of it, because I've met a lot of wonderful people and I've attended lots of the reunions. It's been wonderful. Keeps me young."

For over half a century he collected military artifacts, storing them in his small house. After a lot of hard work negotiating with the town of Cobalt, Jim was offered the use of the vacant Ontario Northland Railway Station. Today this great old building has become a full-scale museum and curator Jones named it "The Bunker." My friend Doug McLellan's mother-in-law lived in nearby New Liskeard and volunteers a few hours a week helping out at the museum. When Doug had a few days off from his editing duties at Global, we headed north to do the story.

Well, we couldn't believe our eyes when we walked through the door. It was without a doubt one of the finest museums we'd ever seen, all done by one man. There was a library and four galleries filled to the rafters with literally thousands of artifacts. There were dozens of mannequins wearing the uniforms of the First and Second World Wars, the Korean War and Vietnam. "To display the uniforms you had to have mannequins," said Jim. "To buy them, it was impossible. I didn't have the money. So I got the notion of making my own. The first few were oddballs; they looked

terrible. But I finally developed a way of doing them and now they're not so bad." In the basement of the old train station, Jim set up a workshop where he builds his mannequins and frames pictures and maps. Almost everything in the Bunker was purchased out of Jim's own pocket. He has had absolutely no government help.

The main gallery in the Bunker is spectacular. It's the largest of the rooms, with a ceiling two stories high, and Jim has hung an open parachute dangling a mannequin in full uniform. Jim's military library consists of more than two thousand books, magazines, and newspaper clippings from World War I to the present day. It's often used by students researching a history project.

The smallest gallery is an English pub. A sign attached to the bar reads: "World War Two pub scene somewhere in England." It came complete with blackout curtains and a group of military men and women standing around a civilian playing the piano. I could almost hear Vera Lynn singing *Now is the Hour* or *A Nightingale Sang in Berkley Square*. This museum is not trying to glorify wa; it's only trying to kindle fond memories.

Jim couldn't run the museum without the help of the many men and women who volunteer, acting as guides and keeping the place shipshape. The day I was doing the story, three lovely ladies were helping out: Maureen Hotts, Doug's mother-in-law, Colleen Belanger, and Nettie Wallman. Nettie brought in some homemade scones and marmalade which we all enjoyed as we got to know each other.

Jim Jones is a very special man. In the summer of 1994, he turned over his entire collection to the town of Cobalt. Quite honestly, I was impressed by this man and his museum.

Photograph courtesy of Aunt Margaret (Patrick) Glover

My grandfather George E. Patrick was a London cigar manufacturer. "Arab" was one of the brands his company made.

CIGAR MAKERS

As a child I was aware that my city grandfather had a cigar factory. I never met Grandpa Patrick, because he passed away when my mother was in her late teens, and I'd never given this bit of knowledge much thought until January of '94, when I received a press release from my old friend Ruth Anne Murray. She works in publicity and promotion for the London Regional Art and Historical Museums and they were having an exhibition about London cigar makers. Ruth Anne and I worked together years ago in London; she was a news reporter at CFPL Radio and I was a news cameraman at CFPL TV. The Wallaceburg native is also sister to one of my best friends, Global news editor Doug McLellan.

When I heard about the exhibition, I decided to do a story on it; I could give it that personal touch because of my grandfather's connection. Before I left for London, I phoned my uncle Ches Patrick in Sarnia to get the exact location of his father's house. He told me the address of the house where he and his two brothers and three sisters, including my mother, had lived. It was 444 Derinda Street in the city's east end. I found a good-looking brick home there, but the two-storey factory out at the back had been torn down and replaced by a standard wooden garage.

In the nineteenth century, London was second only to Montreal as the cigar manufacturing capital of Canada. German immigrants started the business in the 1860s and, by 1914, it had become the largest industry in London, with more than twelve hundred workers, a third of them women. The tobacco used by the London cigar makers wasn't from the fields of nearby Simcoe and Delhi; it came from Cuba. The wrapper leaf was imported from the East Indies. In the museum's collection was a 1913 Vernon's City of London directory and it listed Grandfather George

E. Patrick's original location at 366 Hamilton Road. I drove around to find the building still there, housing a Portuguese shop on its main floor.

At the gallery itself, the exhibition contained a fantastic collection of cigar boxes and cigar-making paraphernalia. Most of the artifacts had been donated by Bob Ward of the William Ward Company, the last cigar factory to close, in 1952. The remainder of the collection came from a local dentist. Of the many handsome cigar boxes, one had come from my grandfather's factory. "Arab" was the brand name on the box.

The numerous wooden boxes, with their gorgeous and sometimes exotic labels, were alone well worth the visit. Cigar maker J. A. Wilson had his own label called "My Own" brand, manufactured expressly for him. "Bell's Special" was manufactured for a local hotel called the Bellview. The "Dolly Varden" was named after a character in a Charles Dickens novel.

Other labels included A.O.K. Cigar, Uneeda Cigar, The Hustler, Marconi, Jack Canuck, Lord Russell and the Highland Lassie; labels display brand names such as Turk, El Imperia, Pan American, Stirton's Dog, and the Clambake Cigar, the last one was manufactured in honour of London's Clambake Club. They were made for an association of hard-drinking travelling salesmen.

Mike Baker, curator of regional history, told me: "Part of the reason cigar making didn't flourish between the First and Second World Wars was that tastes among men changed to cigarettes. It was also a lot easier to carry cigarettes in the trenches because they were in little metal containers as opposed to the big, bulky wooden cigar boxes."

As most youngsters will do, I tried smoking as a boy. I can remember rolling dried maple leaves in the fall, making what looked much like a crude cigar after we'd wrapped them in brown paper. We were lucky we didn't set ourselves ablaze. In my late teens I tried smoking Export and Players cigarettes. They were without filter and we all thought it was cool to tap the ends of your unlit cigarette against the package, making sure the tobacco stayed tight in its paper cylinder. Obviously, I'd seen real men do this.

Not long after I'd struck the match and inhaled a few times, I threw up.

As far as cigars go, it was Old Port rum-dipped with the plastic tip for me and my old friend Tommy Weller. About once a year, I pack my pipe with rich-tasting, even better-smelling pipe tobacco from my father's old humidor, and stand out in front of the garage and puff away. Mind you, it has to be drizzling out, because this way I'm the image of an old fisherman standing at the harbour looking out to sea.

Two London, Ontario Cigar Brands: The Hustler made by Joseph Gasté and Company and Cosmo Panetelas from Wm. Ward and Sons Limited.

OF CITY OF LONDON   639

BELTON Sells The **BEST LUMBER FOR THE LEAST COST**, 2 Yards—Rectory and York; Pall Mall and Richmond

CIGAR MANFRS.

Atkins Wm & Co, 386½ Richmond
Brener Bros, 184-190 Horton
Canada Cigar Co, 67 Bathurst
Donnelly Jas, 310 Cromwell
Dyer Cigar Co, 384 Ridout
Dyer J J & Co, 62 Dundas
El Creo Cigar Co, 185½ Dundas
Gaste J Co, 19 King
Havana Cigar Co Ltd, 421-425 Talbot
Kelly Geo Co, 366 Richmond
Line, McDonald & Co, 346 Clarence
McLeod, Nolan & Co, 422-426 Ridout
McNee J & Sons, 381 Clarence
Manness & Sons, 391 Talbot
Patrick G E, 366 Hamilton rd
Rex Cigar Co, 286-288 Dundas, (see margin lines)
Santa Clara Cigar Co, 257 Wellington
Scout Cigar Co, 90 Stanley
Tuckett Cigar Co Ltd, 334-336 Clarence
Victoria Cigar Co, 591½ Richmond
Ward Wm, 64-66 Dundas

CIVIL ENGINEERS.

Farncomb F W, 402½ Richmond
Moore & Munro, 441½ Richmond

CLOTHING.

(Wholesale & Mnfg)

Britton H A & Co, 85 Dundas
Canadian Overall Co, 98 Carling
Greene-Swift Ltd, 442-450 Talbot
Helena Costume Co, 192-8 King
Ready-to-Wear Ltd, 380 Clarence
Southcott N & Co, 238½ Dundas
Standard Mackintosh Co, 348 Clarence

(Retail)

Andrews' Toggery Ltd, 217 Dundas

Dowler R H & J, 176-78 Dundas
Fashion-Craft, Shop of, 399 Richmond
Fishbein M & Co, 638 Dundas
Grafton & Co Ltd, 158 Dundas
Graham Bros, 157½-9 Dundas and 399 Richmond
Hewitt Geo, 377 Clarence
Kingsmill T F, 130-132 Dundas
Oak Hall, 156 Dundas
Pethick T Co, 386 Richmond
Raphael & Co, 236-238 Dundas
Semi-Ready Tailoring, 182 Dundas
Smallman & Ingram Ltd, 149-57 Dundas and 393-97 Richmond
Standard House Furnishing Co, 656 Dundas
Wegner Clothing Co, 371 Talbot
Wolf Bros, 231 and 658 Dundas
Wolf H & Sons, 265-265½ Dundas
Young R J & Co, 142-144 and 668 Dundas

COAL AND WOOD.

(Wholesale)

Daly J M, 19 York
Heaman Wm & Son, 326 Burwell
Hunt Bros Ltd, 363 Richmond, and 276 Waterloo
Lake Erie Coal Co, 276 Clarence
Mann John & Sons, 401 Clarence
Janes C H & Sons, 711 York
Tilson L E, 580 Talbot
Webster-Harvey Ltd, 185-207 Piccadilly

(Retail)

Boss & Brooks, 274 Maitland
Brooks Bros, 228 Adelaide
Chantler Bros, 263 Bathurst
Connell Anthracite Mining Co, 405 Richmond and 633 Colborne
Daly J M, 19 York
Dominion Coal and Wood Co, 50 Maitland
Gillies D H & Son, 288 Adelaide

Courtesy of London Regional Art and Historical Museums

A page from the 1913 Vernon's City of London directory includes my Grandfather George E. Patrick's original business address.

July 8th, 1939, London England. Sir Harry and Lady Eunice Oakes take a
stroll after receiving his knighthood at Buckingham Palace.

Photograph courtesy of the Museum of Northern History

THE SIR HARRY OAKES CHATEAU

When Harry Oakes stepped down from a passenger traincar at Swastika's railway station, just west of Kirkland Lake, in June of 1911, he had a suitcase in his hand and $2.68 in his pocket. Harry was a prospector and had searched as far away as Australia, California, and Alaska for gold. Now he was going to search around Kirkland Lake. Less than a year later, Harry formed a partnership with the four Tough brothers. The headframe of the Tough-Oakes Mine still stands at the eastern edge of the town. Eventually Harry sold off his shares to the Tough brothers to partially finance what became the Lake Shore Mine. During its peak, it was the largest gold producer in the western hemisphere.

Those were good years and Harry prospered. In 1919, he built a log chateau for his family which was partially destroyed by fire a decade later. Harry wasn't deterred by this disaster and rebuilt his chateau to its current and much grander scale. Today, the incredible structure, with its distinctive copper roof and four fireplaces, is home to the Museum of Northern History. In 1980 the chateau was designated historical by the Ontario Heritage Foundation which recognized the dwelling as the province's best example of prairie-craftsman architecture, a style pioneered by the American architect Frank Lloyd Wright.

The museum is run by a wonderful curator named Lydia Alexander. She and her staff show the museum to over ten thousand visitors annually. On my first meeting with her, she said that I couldn't come back to do the story the next day unless I brought doughnuts. The next morning, I returned at our designated time with two-dozen assorted Tim Horton doughnuts.

"The most important aspect of our museum is the building itself," said Lydia. "The room we're standing in was Harry Oakes' bedroom. You can imagine what it would be like in the morning. He'd roll over in bed and look out the window to see his money making machine . . . right out there." From the bedroom window I was able to photograph the headframe of his mine. Then I set up in daughter Nancy's room, one of the highlights of the chateau due to the designs in the plaster walls. In low-relief, the plasterer had illustrated nursery rhymes, fairy tales, wildlife, and children's toys on the walls. "If you can imagine the changing light in the evening, around sunset," said Lydia, "how it would highlight the figures in relief on these walls."

Every nook and cranny of the chateau is used for visitors or the staff. The children's playroom is now the archives department. There's a small room with glass display cases, filled with stuffed animals. Another room reflects the town's participation in sports. There are rooms filled with displays showing Kirkland Lake's involvement in the mining industry, past and present. Other displays focus on the area's agriculture, timber, and local personalities. A handsome memorial book commemorating Harry's death sits on a desk in the front room. It was produced by the Group of Seven artist A. J. Casson.

On the 8th of July 1939, Harry was knighted at Buckingham Palace. He received his knighthood for making a very large contribution to a London hospital. Eventually, Harry and Eunice left Kirkland Lake to live in Niagara Falls. Then they left Canada and moved to the Bahamas where death caught up with him. Sir Harry Oakes was murdered at the age of sixty-eight. Was it the work of his son-in-law who was charged but aquitted? Was it a Miami mobster whose casino-building plans were opposed by Sir Harry? Did Sir Harry know too much about a wartime plot that involved the Duke and Duchess of Windsor? That murder has never been solved.

The home that Pink Pills built, Fulford Place in Brockville

FULFORD PLACE

The Ontario Heritage Foundation plays a special role in the conservation of our province's heritage. It has the legislated power to hold in trust for the people of Ontario, property of architectural, historical, natural, or archaeological significance.

One such structure is Fulford Place which was bequeathed to the Ontario Heritage Foundation by George Fulford the Second.

The twenty thousand square foot mansion was built by his father, George Taylor Fulford, in 1899. It is one of the few remaining completely intact Edwardian homes in North America. It was financed from profits that George senior made from his "cure-all" remedy known as "Pink Pills for Pale People." George T. Fulford bought the patent to Doctor William's Pink Pills for Pale People from Doctor William Jackson for $53.01 in 1895. He went on to sell millions of boxes of pills around the world, claiming to cure everything from loss of energy to swelling of the legs. The Fulford Company also sold the popular Baby's Own brand of talc and soap, familiar to millions of Canadians.

Originally the property consisted of ten acres and included formal Italian gardens. Sitting on the shoreline of the St. Lawrence River, the family had its own dock, boathouse, and 130-foot steam yacht called *Magedoma.* The staff quarters were bright and modern with hot and cold running water. The family never had a problem hiring or keeping staff.

In his Italian Renaissance dining room, George the First held many important discussions as he established his social and political network. He served as a Brockville City councillor for twelve years, and in 1900 was appointed to the Senate by Sir Wilfrid Laurier. In the library sits a bust of the senator. It was done by Hamilton McCarthy, one of Canada's foremost sculptors at the turn of the century.

In 1880, George married Mary Wilder White, a gracious and popular debutante from Salem, Massachusetts. They had three children: Dorothy, born in 1881, Martha in 1883, and the heir, son George, was born at Fulford Place itself in 1902. Prime Minister Sir Wilfrid and Lady Laurier were visiting George and Mary at the house that very weekend. In Edwardian times, the drawing room was considered the centre of a woman's home. Mary, a gifted pianist, would entertain friends and family there often.

Fulford Place contains thousands of the family's original pieces. Many were collected during their grand tours of the world. There are Oriental ivory carvings and European porcelain. When George passed away in 1905, Mary and her youngest child, Master George, moved south to warmer climates and to be closer to her family in San Diego, California. The staff maintained the propery for their seasonal returns. "The City of Brockville is looking at Fulford Place," said Curator Pam Buell, "as their flagship tourist attraction."

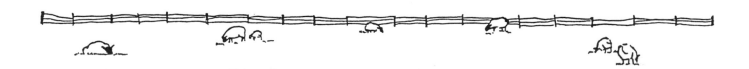

Photograph courtesy of David Lee and Ian Skennerton

James Paris Lee, Wallaceburg inventor of the world-renowned Lee-Enfield
rifle

WALLACEBU... DISTRICT MU...

When my friend Doug McLellan returned to work after a few days off, he was bubbling with excitement about a museum that he'd discovered in his hometown of Wallaceburg. The southwestern Ontario town, with its rich and unique heritage, straddles the banks of the Sydenham River. When the Wallaceburg and District Museum began, the townspeople emptied their attics and garages and found enough artifacts to fill the vacant seven thousand square foot Wallaceburg Hydro building. Since opening day in the early '80s, it has become an important tourist attraction. There are over twenty thousand artifacts housed on three floors, artifacts from the early 1800s to the present day, providing a historical overview of community life. Inside an alarm-triggered glass case rests the world renowned Lee-Enfield Rifle. It was invented in Wallaceburg in 1878 by James Paris Lee. The river-front echoed the very first test shot of this repeater rifle as it whistled across the Sydenham and into an old oak tree on the far side of the river. The British-issued rifle was used in the Boer and the First and Second World Wars. Opera singer Jeanne Gordon was born in Wallaceburg in 1884; she sang at the New York Met and in Europe. The museum has a display of some of Miss Gordon's costumes and photographs.

When I returned to do the story, Doug accompanied me. In one of the display areas set up like an old school classroom, he found his graduation picture in a 1969 high school yearbook. Doug moved away from Wallaceburg a quarter of a century ago but, like most of us who grew up outside the big cities that we end up working in, we still think of these places as home. When we arrived, Doug and I chatted with Marcy Edwards, president of the Historical Society, and Laura Benson, the museum manager. Laura is the only full-time staff member. "I'm sure tha..... ...... can have a connection with Wallaceburg," she said, "if they just open their kitchen cupboard and turn one of their drinking glasses over. They'll probably see the famous Diamond 'D' trademark of our glass factory." The glass industry got its start in Wallaceburg in 1891, and Dominion Glass is still one of the town's major employers. The Wallaceburg Coop-erage Company was one of the first industries, closely followed by such famous names as Wallaceburg Brass, Waltec, the Canada and Dominion Sugar Company and Schultz Die Casting.

The Industry Room contains the world's largest faucet. It was an advertising gimmick for the Wallaceburg Brass Company. The town also manufactures Louisville hockey sticks and Powerbilt golf clubs. Sports have always played an important role in the town's history. Organized lacrosse, for example, started there in 1875. Wallaceburg is the hometown of two NHL players, former Detroit Redwing Dave Kelly and former Toronto Maple Leaf Doug Shedden.

There's a marine room for mahogany boats such as the Mac-Crafts and the Canadian Wildcats were built in this town. In that area you'll see a model of a wheelhouse with vintage shipping artifacts from steamers that came to the town's docks. The area's military heritage is honoured in the Legion Room. Filled with memorabilia, it's dedicated to the many young people who lost their lives during the two World Wars. The Wallaceburg and District Museum is a wonderful example of what volunteer citizens can put together in a community that cares. I could see why my friend Doug was so impressed with this place.

Ska-Nah-Doht (means a village stands again). It's a reconstruction of an Iroquoian Village.

SKA-NAH-DOHT

Driving along Highway 2, just west of Delaware, I spotted a sign for Longwoods Road Conservation Area. An additional sign informed me that there was an Indian village on site as well. I've driven along this stretch many times, but I've never given the roadside sign much thought. After checking in with the lady at the gatehouse, I proceeded into the park. At the resource centre I met Curator Karen Mattila. Karen and Rose Nicholas, a Mohawk and a village intrepreter, took me on a tour of the site. I was impressed with what I saw and made tentative arrangements to come back in the fall.

Ska-Nah-Doht means "a village stands again." And here, twenty miles west of London, a re-creation of an Iroquoian village has been constructed to look as it did a thousand years ago. The Lower Thames Valley Conservation Authority acquired the land in the mid-sixties and erected the village in 1972. That was the year I left CFPL Television in London to take employment with the CBC in Toronto.

The Iroquoians were the first farmers of the area. They built their village on sandy soil, choosing high land near a river. Their main crops were corn, squash, and beans. Because agriculture gave these people a fairly stable food supply, they were able to live in a settlement like this for several years.

"When our school groups come out to the area," said Karen, "Rose and I try to get the children to picture what life would have been like here a one thousand years ago. We try to take their minds back to a time when there was no electricity, no metal shovels or machinery with which to dig the soil for farming. The longhouses and the palisade wall that surrounds the village are all put together by hand. I really think it gives them an idea of what it means to survive."

In those early times, a maze was constructed at the entrance to the village itself. It was designed to slow the enemy down during an attack. The entire village was encircled by a palisade, made of long, slender tree trunks. The palisade provided protection from not only their enemies, but from animals and the wind.

A clan of thirty to fifty people lived in a longhouse. They would all be related through the clan mother. Close to the longhouse, a storage lodge was built to store the communal village property, such as firewood and seed stocks.

Nearby the Indian village is a resource centre, with hands on activities for children. Across from the resource centre, nestled on the edge of the woods, are three log cabins used for workshops and classrooms. The 155 acres of marshland, meadows, and hiking trails are open to the public year round.

HOCKEY NIGHT IN CANADA

GAMES MUSEUM

As children growing up in Lucan, we played marbles, snakes and ladders, croquet, crokinole, table hockey, and the card game fish. We'd play hockey and baseball and, on the Anglican church lawn, we played "English Bulldog Come Across." That had to be a game that had somehow taken root during the war years. When the University of Waterloo sent our assignment desk a news tip about their games museum, I was immediately interested.

The Museum and Archive of Games is housed on campus in the B.C. Matthews Hall. Founded in 1971, the museum is a unique institution dedicated to the collection, exhibition, preservation, and research of games and game-related behaviour. The museum is the only one of its kind in the world, specializing in the collection of games from all time periods and cultures. The current collection totals close to five thousand games and game-related objects. It's managed by the University of Waterloo's Recreation and Leisure Studies Department under Director/Curator Professor Elliot Avedon. "When I was a professor at Columbia University in New York City," said Professor Avedon, "we were studying the meaning of games in society. We wrote to people who sent us examples and explanations. When I came to the University of Waterloo, I had thirty crates of examples." With the help and guidance of the Ontario Government, the professor and the university established the museum.

The exhibit changes every four months. When I was there, the exhibit on display was called "Beyond the Spelling Bee" or "Word Game Revisited." It included more than fifty nineteenth and twentieth century games that challenged a player's command of the alphabet in both French and English. Graduate student Don McLean and Professor Avedon did a visual demonstration for my story of an American game called Gotaminute. The entire game is contained in a clear plastic block which has a one-minute egg-timer and seven lettered cubes. The object of the game was to see how many words you could find on the lettered cubes within the given time.

Graduate students Dave Plouffe and Don McLean operate the museum for the university. They also had on display a truly Canadian game of table hockey. It was invented by Torontonian Donald H. Munro in 1932. The museum's collection ranges from original, one-of-a-kind native Canadian and Inuit games to the latest in computer games. The great thing about the Museum and Archive of Games is that it's open to the public.

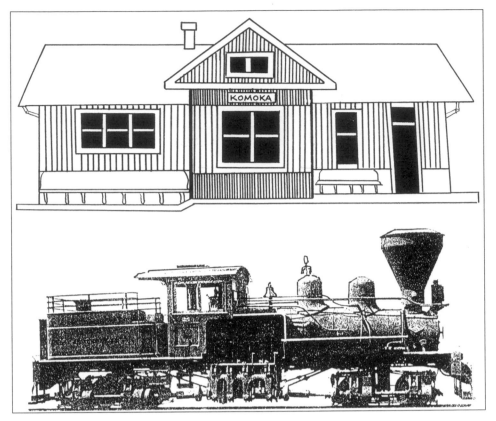

Pen and ink drawing by the author of the former Canadian National Railway Station in Komoka. The 1913 Shay logging locomotive is the museum's pride and joy.

KOMOKA RAILWAY MUSEUM

The first railway went through Komoka in 1854; the Great Western Railroad linked Komoka with Windsor and Niagara Falls. By 1856, a Sarnia branch was completed. Jobs abounded during this construction period. The Great Western Railroad built repair sheds and a roundhouse. At one time the community could boast more than a dozen hotels and taverns. For a while, it was thought that the coming of the railway would make Komoka a thriving city, even bigger than neighbouring London. As a result of this, speculation was rampant and land prices soared. The greed

of a few frightened off many new settlers. When the boom eventually died, London grew and Komoka remained just a small railway settlement.

Today, there are still three rail lines crisscrossing the small southwestern Ontario village, two Canadian National and one Canadian Pacific. But the trains don't stop here anymore. Canadian Pacific demolished its station in 1969, bringing to an end their passenger service. The Canadian National station closed five years later. In 1977, a group of railway buffs calling themselves the Komoka Railway Committee purchased the station from CN for a dollar. This group was headed by local historian and former CN express agent Ron Davis. They trucked the 12 x 45 foot structure over to Komoka Park. Ron, who is now curator of the Komoka Railway Museum, told me, "I just hated to see this opportunity slip by. We've been able to save some of our buildings and part of our historical culture."

The museum would never have opened if it hadn't been for the fantastic support of the men and women volunteers who have spent thousands of hours building this museum. The day I was shooting my story, I met Raymond Leach, Martin Van Meyel, Cec Bowes, and Jamie Forsythe who were busy laying some track. A good many of the volunteers are retired, but not Jamie. He's a grade twelve student from Strathroy and he is nuts about trains.

"It's always fun coming out and hanging around with these guys," Jamie said. "It's kind of funny because, on Saturdays when I show up, they'll always have a smile on their faces, because I usually end up doing the heavy work. I don't mind driving spikes and stuff like that; it keeps me busy on weekends."

The volunteers have constructed an enormous driveshed housing a 1913 Shay logging locomotive. Shay #2679 was built in Lima, Ohio. First owned by the Dennis Lumber Company, the engine spent its entire life in Canada working in the Algonquin Park area, transporting logs to the saw mill. A total of 3354 Shay engines were built; today there are only thirty left worldwide.

The walls of the driveshed are lined with railway memorabilia. There are signal lights and crossing signs. Ron Davis's own collection of railway lanterns is neatly displayed along one wall. You'll find a three-wheel velocipede, which is an early form of a handcar, and there's a motorized jigger. The museum owns hundreds of photographs the steam era, many of which can't be displayed bec there's not enough room. Sitting alongside the station is one of their latest acquisitions, a seventy-foot-long, seventy-tonne baggage car. It was built for Canadian National Railway in 1939.

The station itself looks much as it did when it was in use by CN. The interior is in mint condition and brought back memories of when I was a youngster leaving my village of Lucan station to go to Sarnia. One of the three rooms has been set up with an operating model railway. The HO gauge electric trains speed along a train board that was designed and constructed to look like Komoka itself. Cec Bowes, the museum president, was operating it with the help of his enthusiastic grandson, Jamie Katenberg. The dream of these dedicated rail buffs is to erect another building large enough to house a theatre and a library. They also hope one day to acquire a boxcar and a caboose.

To help raise funds to keep the museum going, they hold pancake breakfasts, flea markets, and ham and turkey Easter bingos. The museum is always willing to accept railway-related items, books and, of course, monetary donations.

December 1994 was an exciting month for Ron Davis. The museum got its very first grant in the form of a three thousand dollar cheque from the Ontario Government's Culture and Recreation department, and Ron retired. He was a custodian for thirty years at Parkview Public School in Komoka. He helped plant the grass when the school was first constructed. Now, the man who seems to run more than he walks can spend all his time being the curator of the Komoka Railway Museum. That is, as long as Mrs. Davis doesn't mind.

Photograph: Brian Morin/Parks Canada

Fort St. Joseph, St. Joseph Island. Looking across the remains of the guardhouse (1799), towards the St. Mary's River.

FORT ST. JOSEPH

In the 1790s, a British Army Lieutenant called Fort St. Joseph, "the military Siberia of Upper Canada." It was so far from civilization that soldiers would pray not to be posted there. The lonely site sits high above the St. Mary's River at the southeastern tip of St. Joseph Island. Today the fort, roughly eighty km from Sault Ste. Marie, is a National Historic Park run by Parks Canada. Fort St. Joseph was established in 1796, the end of the defence line which the British built across their colonies to protect them from American attack. By 1803, the blockhouse, guardhouse, and powder magazine were completed. The fort was also the western headquarters of the British Indian Department and a major fur trade supply depot. It safeguarded the trade route from Montreal to the Upper Great Lakes. Once it was established, the Montreal merchants, who had continued to trade at the American Fort Michilimackinac, followed the British to Fort St. Joseph. They erected huts, stores, and wharves and it wasn't long before a full-scale village emerged.

The Indian Department at the fort strengthened accord with the Ojibwa. This alliance served the British well on the outbreak of the War of 1812. On the 16th of July, 1812, British soldiers, along with fur traders and native allies, left Fort St. Joseph for Fort Michilimackinac which they captured without bloodshed. The British garrison, the Indian Department, and many of the fur traders then transferred to that fort. Two years later, the Americans took revenge and burned Fort St. Joseph to the ground. At the end of the war, the British handed Fort Michilimackinac back to the Americans. The British then built a post on nearby Drummond Island. About the same time, the Montreal merchants and the fur traders lost their trading privileges south of the Great Lakes, so they abandoned St. Joseph Island. Fort St. Joseph was never rebuilt.

Every morning, from Victoria Day to Thanksgiving Day weekend, Jennifer Corbett, Chief of Visitor Services, hoists an old Union-Jack over the fort ruins. "A lot of visitors come here expecting to see a fully reconstructed fort," said Jennifer. "We try to explain that the site is an archaeological one. Parks Canada is not going to reconstruct it, they're going to continue to excavate."

After my interview with Jennifer, I shot scenes of this important part of Canadian history. You can still see the remains of the guardhouse, built in 1799, and the thick walls of the powder magazine which stored the black powder used in firearms. As you wander the ruins at your own pace, panels explain what each building had been. The ground floor of the blockhouse was used for storing supplies, while the second storey provided accommodation. The building was so poorly constructed that the rain and snow blew in through the cracks in the log walls. Even ink froze in the wintertime.

As you wander the grounds, it's not hard to visualize what life must have been like in this desolate outpost. Fort St. Joseph is by no means all outdoors; they have a very impressive visitors, centre, including a film theatre. Many of the archaeological artifacts found at the fort are on display here. There are also extremely helpful and knowledgeable interpreters. The day I was there, a young woman named Siobhan Fagan was an enormous help to me.

Don't expect Old Fort Henry, because it's not. But it's sure worth a visit if you're planning a trip to the Sault Ste. Marie area. Standing among the ruins, looking out across the St. Mary's River, the scene is much as it was two hundred years ago.

JOHN AND HARMKE WORK WITH CARE.
HE FIXES CARS AND SHE FIXES HAIR.

CAR AND HAIR CARE

Occasionally, finding the exact address can be a bit tricky, so I tend to give myself extra time when I'm heading out to do a story. I've always taken pride in being on time as I travel distances of two and more hours. What may be a familiar landmark or signpost to the folks that give me directions can sometimes be hard for a newcomer to find. One cold, wet morning in the spring of '94, I was searching Highway 6, south of Durham, for a sign marking the 14th concession of Eggermont Township. I was headed for the home and studio of folk artist Mary Jo Pinder. My instructions were, "If you get to Varney, you've gone too far."

As I drove smack, dab into the middle of this tiny Grey County hamlet, I spotted a garage. The lads who work in garages are always a wealth of information. I'll bet they've even made a service call or two out that way. Through the downpour, I rushed from my station wagon.

As I entered by the office door, I stood dumfounded. Surprise, surprise—I had walked right into a beauty salon, complete with hairdresser giving a perm. "Are you looking for the garage or would you like your hair done?" said the stylist. "'Cause if you're going to the garage, it's right through that door over there, okay?" I couldn't believe my eyes. After excusing myself to the ladies, I made my way out to the garage. I guess in my mad dash through the rain, I hadn't seen the sign outside.

It turns out that this unusual enterprise is owned by John and Harmke Hoekstra. They call it Varney Car and Hair Care. The car care is a general service garage, and John, along with his right-hand man, Daniel Sowiluk, specializes in brakes, exhaust, and suspensions. The beauty shop is operated by John's wife, Harmke.

Sitting under the dryer was Harmke's first steady customer, Muriel Hartwick. After retirement, the Northern Telecom employee moved from the bustling metropolis of Acton to the slower pace of Varney. By the way, Harmke has been a stylist all her working career. She opened her first shop in Strathroy when she was just seventeen years old. In the main beauty shop chair sat Mary Jo Sowiluk. She's another regular and married to Daniel, the mechanic in the garage.

I asked John and Harmke what kind of reactions they receive from first-time visitors. "When they walk into the beauty shop, they always walk right back out," said Harmke. "They think they're in the wrong place. But they come on through, and I tell them that I'll give them a haircut on the way out if they like."

"When my wife is gone to town to pick up automotive parts for me," John said, "people come in for a haircut and they say, 'Well who's going to do the hair?' I'll say, well I can, I can get my side cutters or tin snips and we'll fix you right up quick." We all laughed.

What does their first steady customer have to say about all this? "I come every Thursday to get my hair done, and if I need my car serviced," said Muriel, "I can have it serviced while I'm having a wash and set."

It was a couple of months before I returned to do the story with John and Harmke. And when I arrived, I noticed the couple had repainted the front of their garage and re-lettered the beauty shop sign. They told me that they'd tidied it up a bit, because they knew I was coming. The Hoekstras have a motto for their business: John and Harmke work with care. He fixes cars and she fixes hair.

CYCLING CANADA

I was driving south along Highway 404, to our studios in Don Mills, when I heard an odd interview on CBC's *Morningside*. Peter Gzowski was interviewing a man who was cycling across Canada. What made this live interview so strange was that the chap talking to Peter was cycling across Canada in the middle of the winter. He was calling from some remote spot in Newfoundland. As I listened, it became evident that the cyclist was not suffering from chills or frostbite because he was making the entire trip in the basement of his home. Hugh Marchand was peddling an exercise bike from St. John's, Newfoundland to Vancouver, British Columbia in the warmth and coziness of his house in Bolton, Ontario. It wasn't hard to track down Hugh through the phone book, and he was very receptive to doing a story with me.

It all began for the fifty-two-year-old business consultant as a New Year's resolution to keep fit. Armed with a goal and identifying the steps to achieve it, Hugh devised his game plan. On the 3rd of January, 1993, Hugh began his imaginary journey. He must average eleven and a half miles every day in order to arrive in Vancouver by the 31st of December that same year. "If you want to simulate the journey," said Hugh, "you look at the terrain you're going through and if you're heading into hilly country, you have to be honest with yourself and crank up the tension on your exercise bike." Hugh has driven across Canada by automobile three times, so he knows the country well. Every day, he punches his mileage into the computer, keeping an accurate log of how far he's travelled in total. There are days when he'll peddle more than his required amount in order to bank mileage. This allows for downtime and holidays. With large, full-scale maps pinned to his basement walls, Hugh marks off his journey as he passes through the various Canadian hamlets, villages, and towns.

What do his three children think? They're very supportive and think it's great that he's made a game out of his exercise program. Hugh's wife has become involved. She started in February from Vancouver and, because she has to climb through the Rockies near the beginning of her trip, he teased her that they'd cross paths in Calgary. Hugh's imaginary bicycle journey will take him through some of the most beautiful parts of our country. The day I did the story with Hugh, heavy snow was falling. Standing in front of my television camera, with large snowflakes landing on me, I spoke these words: "Hugh is taking the northerly route across Canada and won't be coming through his hometown. As a matter of fact, ninety days from now, he'll be somewhere near Kirkland Lake in the middle of black-fly season. I'm Terry Culbert for Global News in Bolton, Ontario."

By May 20th, Hugh cycled into Matheson, Ontario, which is almost due north of Bolton. The prediction I made in my story was not that far out. In late June, Hugh received a letter from Laura Jefferson, a Vancouver teacher who had been listening to the CBC *Morningside* broadcasts about his trip. She'd decided to make him her class project. Each week Hugh would fax Laura a bulletin describing the terrain and towns he was passing through. The children in turn sent him posters and letters of encouragement. Laura told Hugh that teaching geography that year had never been easier.

By August he had made such good progress that he was able to take a two-week holiday with his family to visit his Mom in England. It was her eightieth birthday. When they returned from their trip, Hugh got back at it. By October 16th, he'd crossed the Continental Divide into British Columbia. Hugh told me that it felt like he'd been pedalling uphill for months. "One of the problems of a stationary bike," he said, "is that you have to pedal downhill as well. There's no coasting." Over the next two months, Hugh threw his back out as he slipped getting out of the shower and, a month before Christmas, the pedal mounting which is welded to the frame, detached itself. Bolted into place, the pedal now caused slippage and, as a consequence, his average speed began to fall. He still had 274 miles to go.

Hugh wanted to finish the trip off on a real bicycle. He wanted to pedal that bike right to the edge of Pacific Ocean. Determined to do this, he was able to arrange a business trip to Vancouver for December 12th. On his stationary bike he pedalled to within twelve miles of his destination. Laura Jefferson, the Vancouver teacher, and her father Jack heard of his plan and offered accommodation and a mountain bike for the last lap. CBC's *Morningside* was aware of Hugh's plans and had delivered a cellular phone to the Jeffersons, so they could interview him during the final dramatic moments. Hugh arrived in Vancouver on the 12th and spent a very pleasant weekend with the Jeffersons as they mapped out the final dozen miles.

Then, Monday morning arrived. With the time difference between Vancouver and Toronto where *Morningside* originates, Hugh and Jack had to get up really early. They drove to False Creek, which would give Hugh a twelve-mile mountain bike ride to the finish line. CBC Radio called and they had their first interview of that day. Peter Gzowski was away, so Hugh talked to guest host Liz Palmer. After the phone interview, Hugh set off. He battled gale-force winds as he cycled along the shoreline path past Granville Island.

At Granville Bridge, Jack, who'd been following in his 4x4, persuaded him to stop for a picture.

Forty minutes ahead of schedule, Hugh rode the bike to the appointed spot, on the beach below the English Bay Cafe. Then it was time to talk to Liz Palmer at *Morningside* again.

While she was doing the second interview, Hugh rode his bike across the promenade, past a sign which read "No Cycling" and then finally onto the beach. Liz said she thought there were still many people, some even in the CBC control room, who didn't believe he was actually there. After all, Hugh had faked his cycle ride for the past year from his basement. So, he held the cellular phone down low so she could hear the sound of the waves. Then the final moment: "So here I am," said Hugh, "a mare usque ad mare." Hugh told me that he'd rehearsed that line. He went on to tell the *Morningside* audience: "My front wheel is in the Pacific Ocean and my sneakers are soaking wet." As Jack popped flash photos like a veteran news photographer, Liz asked Hugh what he had planned to do as an encore? "We now have a treadmill in our basement and I still have an old rowing machine," he told her. "I thought I'd follow the route of the voyageurs and explorers and canoe and portage across the country." Liz replied: "You should see the faces of the people in the control room. They're going nuts."

Hugh told me that it was truly wonderful to hear this comment from Liz, because he'd spoken to so many of CBC Radio's technical people during the broadcast setups throughout the year. Hugh said that they were a really great bunch of people.

Monday, December 13th, 1993. Jack Jefferson persuaded Hugh to stop for a photograph near the Granville Island Bridge, forty minutes before he dipped his feet into the Pacific Ocean.

Photograph courtesy of Willy Nelson (1993)

William E. (Willy) Nelson, president of Universal Wax of Perth, Ontario. Willy is standing in front of Chernobyl's number four reactor which exploded and burned in 1986.

THE WAX MAN OF PERTH

During the dreadful cold snap of January '94, I was in the Ottawa Valley area doing three stories. On the first day out, I did a story on General Store Publishing House in the hamlet of Burnstown near Renfrew. This is the publishing firm that produced the book you're holding in your hands. On the second day, I went to the Word Farm, forty-five minutes east of Ottawa. The husband and wife team of Gisele Grignon and Morley Seaver had left the nation's capital with their children to start a business in the country. After doing the story and having lunch with Gisele and Morley, I headed west on Highway 417 for Ottawa. I was in time to listen to one of my favorite CBC Radio programs, *Gabereau*. Vicki Gabereau's guest was a man named Willy Nelson, not the singer, but the wax man from Perth, Ontario. I scratched down a few points in my trusty reporter's notepad as I drove. Willy told Vicki that he'd been invited by the Ukrainian government to see if he could help stop the leak of radiation at the nuclear reactor at Chernobyl.

From the time I heard Willy until the date I'd set up to meet him at his lab in Perth, he travelled to Russia twice. The self-taught wax technician and environmentalist is confident that paraffin wax can stop radiation leaks in the cracked sarcophagus that contains the stricken reactor. Willy showed me a letter from the Russian authorities asking him back. The officials told him that he was the first person to come to them with something useful. "My wax will solve four of the main problems," said Willy. "It will solidify airborne dust and solidify dust inside the sarcophagus. The wax will prevent water from leaking into the sarcophagus walls, then down into the basement. It could be used to prevent further rusting of the steel structure and pipes within the sarcophagus. And I've invented a membrane that could be used for reclaiming polluted land. It would cost about sixteen cents an inch, but it would enable the people to grow food again." For an experiment on his second visit, Willy laid a 15 x 30 foot membrane down in back of a Chernobyl home, covered the membrane in pollution-free topsoil and planted with seeds. When he returns for a third visit, he'll be able to assess the membrane's effectiveness.

At twelve, Willy was making candles of wax and by the late fifties he'd found that wax could be used to reduce air pollution from automobiles and chimney stacks. The scientific world doesn't always take him seriously, as he has no formal training, although there are scientists who think he doesn't get the recognition he deserves. When the American oil tanker *Exxon Valdez* ran aground off Alaska in 1989, he offered his services. Exxon said, "no thanks." This sort of negative response upsets the wax man from Perth. In his lab, Willy demonstrated on camera for me exactly how his wax process works. He knows that his system would have been useful in the *Exxon Valdez* crisis and that it would have cost a fraction of what they spent. He also strongly believes that most of the wildlife could have been spared.

For the past fifteen years, IGI International Waxes of Toronto has provided Willy with wax at no charge because they believe in him. He's had absolutely no financial support from the Canadian government. School classes frequently stop by to see Willy as he demonstrates the importance of wax. His long-term goal is to build an institute of wax technology, "a school for the betterment of mankind," he calls it. Willy's not looking for praise or recognition; he gives all the credit to wax, which has been around for millions of years.

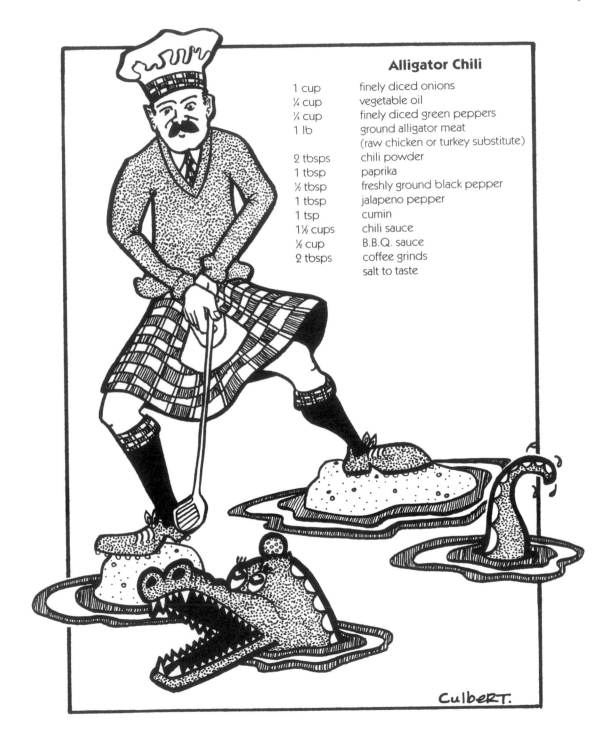

Alligator Chili

1 cup	finely diced onions
¼ cup	vegetable oil
¼ cup	finely diced green peppers
1 lb	ground alligator meat
	(raw chicken or turkey substitute)
2 tbsps	chili powder
1 tbsp	paprika
⅛ tbsp	freshly ground black pepper
1 tbsp	jalapeno pepper
1 tsp	cumin
1⅛ cups	chili sauce
⅛ cup	B.B.Q. sauce
2 tbsps	coffee grinds
	salt to taste

Culbert.

THE GOLFING CHEF

If Jim Law had discovered golf before he became a gourmet chef, he'd probably be on the professional golf circuit right now. Born in Dundee, Scotland, Jim spent his early years travelling the high seas as chef in the merchant marine. This experience not only broadened his horizons and palate, but it also provided him with a wealth of humorous stories. During his fourteen-year career on board various ships, his travels took him to many of the world's most beautiful golf courses. So what more appropriate spot to go as a landlocked chef when he left the merchant marine than St. Andrews, Scotland, where golf began? While working as head chef for Rufflets Hotel, the 1969 British Open was played almost on his doorstep. That event became the catalyst that led to Jim's enduring fascination with the game.

In 1972 Jim emigrated to Canada. In his newly adopted country he received his papers as a secondary school teacher in the art of cuisine. In the early '80s he took a part-time position as a chef at The Feathers Pub in Toronto's east end. During that summer I met Jim, as I'm a partner in this British-style pub on Kingston Road. He was hired by my good friend Ian Innes, a fellow Scot and golf enthusiast. Originally from Edinburgh, Ian is the chief partner and general manager of The Feathers. During Jim's summer employment, he and Ian were known to play a few rounds of golf together.

Over the next few years, Jim's passion for cooking and playing golf led to him writing a cookbook. In the spring of 1993, *Putter A Round (in your kitchen) with the Golfing Gourmet* was published. It's an eclectic mix of recipes and cooking tips interspersed with stories about his escapades in the merchant marine and on the golf course. Visually, this cookbook made a good television story. I was able to photograph Jim on the golf course and then in the kitchen. For the two-minute feature he cooked up a southern recipe called "Alligator Chili." Jim uses farm-raised alligator, not the meat of reptiles poached from the wild. A substitute would be raw ground turkey or chicken. "Chicken's a great substitute", said Jim, "but it just doesn't have the bite, if you know what mean."

Jim is a member of the Escoffier Society and the Canadian Federation of Chefs de Cuisine. It is also verified that, on the 5th of June 1985, Jim got his first hole-in-one at the Whitevale Golf Club near Pickering, Ontario.

September 7th 1994. Jethro the duck with its adopted family, Kevin, Mary Anne holding Jethro, Stephanie and Dr. Jeff Silver.

JETHRO THE LUCKY DUCK

Global anchorman Peter Kent stopped me in the hallway at work. He'd been listening to a noon-hour radio show on CFRB, and heard a veterinarian tell the story of a little duckling that his children had saved. Peter, always a good source for story ideas, thought this one would be of interest to me. I thanked him, and proceeded to track down the Dr. Jeff Silver, a veterinary surgeon living in Thornhill. He told me that the summer of '94 started off like most for his children Stephanie and Kevin. They were holidaying at the family cottage on Gull Lake near Minden, when something wonderful happened. His children were out exploring a little island with their dog Boomer when they came across a bird's nest on the ground. The eggs were scattered all about. Gently, the children placed the eggs back in the nest, hoping that the mother would return. As they set the individual eggs back, they noticed that one had a crack and a piece of shell missing from it. Kevin and Stephanie brought the egg home for dad to examine. When it was discovered that the membrane was intact, the family incubated the egg with towels and hot-water bottles. The tender loving care worked. At five o'clock on the morning of July the 29th, baby Jethro was born. From the very beginning, Mary Anne, the children's mother, began documenting the tiny creature on home video. Jethro was treated like a star celebrity.

I caught up with the Silvers at their Thornhill home. Dr. Silver had made a box for Jethro to live in while they were back in the city. "I believe it's a misconception that animals, once touched by humans," he said, "will not be accepted by their parents again. I would like to stress that that's a misconception. If a small bird falls from a nest, or you find a little baby squirrel and know where the mother is, the mother will accept the animal back to be raised naturally, even though the scent of humans might be on it."

At six weeks, Jethro thinks of the Silver family as his own. I guess they're sort of his mom, dad, sister, and brother. He follows them everywhere.

The Silver family knew that they wouldn't be able to keep Jethro forever, so they made arrangements with the town of Richmond Hill for his release. When Jethro is old enough, he'll be placed in Mill Pond. If he decides not to fly south for the winter with the other ducks, the parks department promised to look after him.

SOLAR NUT

There's a pretty darn good chance that I wouldn't have done this story if it hadn't been brought to my attention by Global cameraman Kevin Smith. Kevin lives in Roches Point, where Cook's Bay and Lake Simcoe meet. Kevin found the story of a local man who was into solar photography in a big way. Kevin's community newspaper, the *Georgina Advocate,* reported that this chap had even built his own observatory.

John Hicks started his working career with Dow Chemical after graduating from Ryerson. When he realized that wasn't his calling, he went back to school. Graduating from the University of Toronto in landscape architecture, he's now self-employed designing parks. Two days a week he teaches at Sir Sandford Fleming in Lindsay. John spends all his spare time studying the star that gives us life.

Most people take the sun for granted. It rises at dawn in the east and goes down at dusk in the west. "No big deal," some might say. But, to John, it's one of the most important things there is. As a matter of fact, taking pictures through his American-made 3000 mm telescope has provided John with many award-winning photographs. And the solar photographer is only an amateur astronomer.

John got the astronomy bug in 1978 while standing on his back porch looking at the milky way. Sixteen years later, at fifty-four, the Toronto native is calling himself a solar nut. "I find that time flies by very quickly when I'm in my observatory," he says. " Three hours can literally seem like three minutes."

John began by studying the stars, but it's the sun that really fascinates him. "I study the sun because it's an object I can look at during the daytime," he said. "And because there are probably few people studying the sun, it gives me a little bit of singularity which I also enjoy. There's been a lot of progress made in deep-sky photography in the amateur astronomy world. I wanted to make that sort of impact in solar astronomy." This is an interesting solar fact that I received from John: if you were a passenger in a modern aircraft flying at a speed of five hundred miles per hour, you would reach the outer surface of the sun in approximately twenty-one years. And that's only if your aircraft could survive the heat of the corona, one million degrees K.

His solar photography appears with regularity in two American publications. Canada's leading astronomy writer, Terence Dickinson, gave John a full page in his book, *The Backyard Astronomer's Guide*. When the book came out, I did a story with Terence at his home in Eastern Ontario. That was in 1991.

Not all John's observing is done from his backyard observatory. On July 11, 1991, the day of the Big One, he was in Mexico to take pictures of the solar eclipse. Along with friends and members of the Royal Astronomical Society, he flew into a small desert town called Santiago. It is located fifty km north of Los Cabos in the southern tip of Baja. In spite of extremely hot temperatures, the event was a tremendous experience, although John was heard to say to a friend, "It was one beautiful eclipse, Doug, but I'd sure as hell hate to live here." After designing and building his own observatory, he now markets the building plans to amateur astronomers all over the world.

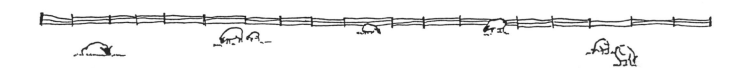

DIVINING

Almost every city, town, and village is on a community water supply. This is not the case if you live in a rural area. Folks out on the farm or in new houses that have been built in the country must drill for their drinking water on their own property. Sometimes the well driller has to go quite deep to find the source. How do they go about finding the right spot to drill? Well, some companies still believe in an old-fashioned method called divining or water witching. There are skeptics that dismiss this practice as hocus-pocus, but there are true believers, like Brent Stainton. He's the owner of Stainton Well Drilling and Pump Equipment just north of London. "I use witching ninety-nine percent of the time before taking our rigs out," Brent said. "I find that it's better than a shot in the dark."

The man Brent uses is Caradoc Township farmer, Ivan Linton. The Strathroy area man has a darn good record of finding underground water veins since 1946. That's the year his father hired a diviner to find water on their family farm. Ivan, along with his dad and brother, was intrigued by what this chap was doing. As they watched and studied the diviner's technique, they all became aware that they had the gift to do it too. "I don't particularly care for the term witching," said Ivan. "I'm not magic and there's no psychic or special powers involved. I don't cast spells or anything. I'm just an ordinary guy who has the gift to find water."

I set up my tripod and camera a good distance back from where Ivan was about to search. As he made his way across the farm field, he was gripping a curved piece of Number 9 wire. As he walked, he concentrated in silence. All the while his eyes were fixed on that piece of wire. Suddenly, it happened. The wire turned away from him and swung towards the ground. Ivan believes a magnetic field is set up by the moving underground water. He feels his ability to conduct electricity triggers this reaction. Not only does Ivan locate the water, he can also estimate how deep the drillers will have to go down. Picking up a piece of straight wire, he knelt down in the grass and held the wire by one end and counted the bounces. Each bounce represented one foot.

The big thrill was when he allowed me to give it a try. I even set up my camera to capture this. With Ivan firmly holding the wire, I gripped a pair of plicrs at one end of the rod. Then we began to walk. It was unbelievable. As we approached the underground water source, the wire began to turn downwards. With all my might, holding the pliers, I couldn't stop the wire turning downwards. There was no hocus-pocus in what I felt and witnessed with my own eyes, and the camera recorded it all. I must admit that I was impressed with Ivan Linton, the man who calls himself just an ordinary guy.

Photo: George Mathewson/The Observer

Dianne Simms was the first and only woman to captain a CN Ferry across the mile-wide St. Clair River between Sarnia, Ontario and Port Huron, Michigan.

FEMALE FERRY CAPTAIN

As I stood alongside the tracks that led to the ferry dock, I was waiting to meet Canadian National Railways' first woman ferry captain, Dianne Simms. Her job was to transport traincars on a huge barge across the St. Clair River from Sarnia to Port Huron, Michigan. I don't know what I was expecting, but it sure wasn't this petite and very attractive lady, who got out of her car and asked me if I was Terry from Global News. She was wearing designer bib-overalls and a hand-knit sweater, make-up and earrings, and she looked more like she was going out on a date than starting her early morning shift as the skipper of the

twenty-year-old tug, the *Phyllis Yorke*. We walked down the dock along the full length of the barge attached to the bow of her tug. "My dad was a captain here for eight years," she said. "He's the one who inspired me to start as a deckhand. I've been doing that for the past five years and I've always felt that I could work in the wheelhouse as well. I thought it would be a challenge."

Up in the wheelhouse I shot scenes of Dianne at work. When the barge was loaded with specially designed train-cars containing a cargo of new automobiles, Dianne powered up her three diesel engines. She had just under three thousand horsepower at her fingertips. Piloting the tug and barge, with an overall length of five hundred feet, is quite a challenge for Dianne; it's quite a challenge for any of the shipmasters who captain either of the two CN ferries. The St. Clair River between Sarnia and Port Huron is a mile wide. It was winter when I did Dianne's story and there was ice in the river.

"As we're approaching the dock," she said, "my deckhand will help me into the slip. There's a camera up forward and, as I watch the monitor, I can see how close I am with my distance and speed. One of the things I have to determine are the winds and the currents."

As we entered the American dock, another woman was preparing to offload the cargo. Sonia Hartley's job as a deckhand was to keep an exact record of everything that comes on or goes off the vessel. Once docked in the United States, Sonia works with employees of the Grand Trunk Railway. In 1992, Canadian National had a record January and February, transport 13,504 railway cars across the St. Clair River. The CN ferry service went into operation in 1971 and it's a seven-day-a-week, twenty-four-hour-a-day operation.

"Summertime is the most challenging time of the year to skipper the ferry across," said Dianne, "because you have to deal with river traffic, like the small fishermen. They're everywhere. Then there are the major ships as well. The great lake freighters are constantly coming up and down the river. Plus, you always have to deal with the weather, and this time of year, it's ice and heavy winds."

Canadian National's cargo is ninety percent automobile related, from parts to brand-new vehicles. CN also transports newsprint, building materials, and it always fascinates Dianne when part of their shipment is airplane wings. There you had all three forms of transportation in one: a train carrying an airplane on a boat.

Once back on the Canadian side, I bid farewell to Dianne and wished her well. As I got behind the wheel of my Global station wagon, I thought that parking an automobile must be a breeze after a day with the *Phyllis Yorke.*

Well, Dianne Simms and the CN ferry service are now history because they've built a new railway tunnel under the St. Clair River. Why did they have to build a new rail passage under the international waterway? Because many of the modern double-stack container and multi-level auto carrier trains are just too large for the existing nineteenth century tunnel. The tunnel will help to speed up the movement of goods shaving twelve hours off the time it took to barge the trains across the river.

Dianne and her colleagues knew that there would be a loss of many railway jobs, so she went looking and found a new one. Dianne's last day with CN was March 16th, 1993. The next day she was with the Canadian Coast Guard as a marine traffic regulator. From an office complex in downtown Sarnia, Dianne monitors all American, Canadian, and foreign vessels over twenty metres in length as they travel from Lake St. Clair, down the Detroit River, the Rouge River, then out into Lake Erie. Long Point is their last call in to Sarnia before Dianne hands them off to Seaway Welland.

She issues and distributes information that is pertinant to the safety of navigation. This includes radioing the ships that a lighted buoy may be off position or adrift, letting the ships know of anything adrift, from a small boat to a floating picnic table, or any diving operations taking place.

Dianne is a third-generation sailor. Her father, Captain Lloyd Simms, retired in 1991, but still works part-time, operating a small tug called *Glenada* out of Sarnia. He transfers pilots to the saltwater vessels above the Bluewater Bridge in Lake Huron.

Dianne's grandfather, John Simms, was captain of a private seventy-foot schooner called *Chimon.* It was owned by the Timothy Eaton family.

CFPL Televison Newsreel Cameraman Jack Schenck, filming London's Santa Claus Parade. I shot this photograph in the early 1960s. Jack was positioned above the entranceway to the now torn-down Hotel London.

NEWSREEL CAMERAMAN RETIRES

Basically self-taught, my friend and colleague Jack Schenck of London, Ontario has retired. After thirty-five years as a news cameraman with CFPL Television, known now as TV London, Jack has handed in his camera gear. His interest in photography began at the age of twelve. The drug-store in his hometown of Stratford did such a poor job of developing his roll of film that he went out and purchased his own darkroom equipment. This was the beginning of a life long career in photography. Eventually he became a still photographer with the *Stratford Beacon Herald*. Then, the big city beckoned, and he was hired by the *London Free Press*. When Walter J. Blackburn, owner/publisher of the *London Free Press*, built and opened CFPL television, Jack was offered a position as a newsreel cameraman. He turned it down, fearing that television wasn't here to stay. That was 1953. "I really didn't think television would last," said Jack. "There was a world of difference between still photography and motion picture."

Jack did change his mind, and over the next three and a half decades, he shot thousands of daily news stories. From bank robberies to fall fairs, from military manoeuvers to celebrities and prime ministers. I remember working as Jack and Lloyd Gatland's soundman when we covered London's Santa Claus Parade. I worked with them a couple of years in a row. The parade, like everything else in those days, was shot on 16 mm black and white film. After the parade was over, the film had to be processed and edited.

Jack and reporter Bill Kearns received the National Headliners Award for outstanding achievement in television news reporting. The award was given for a four-minute film they did in Montreal titled *Expo 67's Dying Hours*.

Jack is a perfectionist in every way. He's also a patient man who taught me a lot about my craft when I was a rookie film cameraman during the 1960s and '70s. CFPL TV was a wonderful shop in which to work and learn your trade. Almost all the cameramen had been newspaper photographers, because television was just an infant in Canada when they all started. Ron Laidlaw was the longest-serving News Director, retiring just before Jack. He was part of the team that put the station on the air. Ron had been with the *London Free Press* and overseas with the RCAF as a photographer during the war. He was more like a father-figure to me and put up with a lot of my so-called artistic temperaments during those early days. Ken Dougan, assistant news director, had been a newspaper photographer and World War Two army photographer. Scottish-born George Rennie, a gruff, tough newsman with a heart of gold, was from newspaper. Lloyd Gatland, an Ingersoll native, had been a still photographer. When it came to composing pictures and teaching a young aspiring cameraman the tricks of the trade, these men were the best.

Jack and his wife Florrie have been married for over forty years. They're grandparents and parents to a registered nurse and a aerospace engineer. When I asked Jack about retirement plans, he said: "I'm going to finish building my French design Jodel single-wing aircraft and take Florrie on at least one good trip a year." Happy retirement Jack, to both of you. And thanks for being a patient teacher.

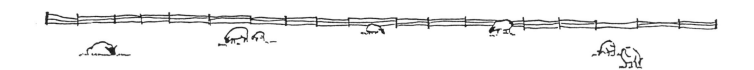

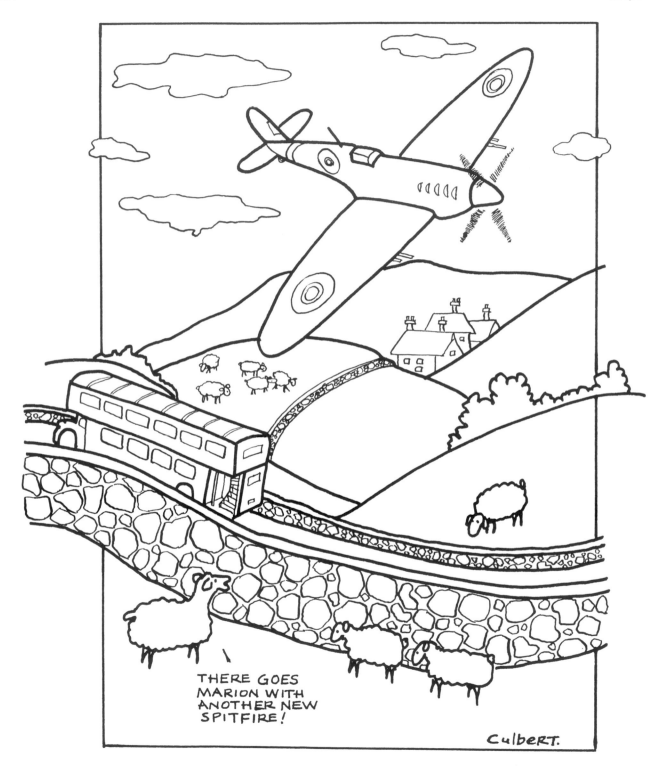

MARION ORR THE PILOT

As a member of the Unionville District Veterans Association, my membership card has allowed me to stop in and quaff a pint at a number of Royal Canadian Legions throughout the province. When you're on the road, on your own as I am, sometimes the four walls of the motel room seem to close in, and as a rule the local Legion Hall is a pleasant place to visit. I take my notes and information along from that day's story and work on my script. It was early in the spring of '91 when I was on an overnighter in Huron County. That evening after supper, I visited the Legion Hall in Clinton where I sat in their lounge area with my beer and started to thumb through a magazine called *Airforce*. I came across a great article by Doug Stuebing titled: "21,000 HRS at the controls." It was the story of a five-foot four-inch, seventy-one-year-old woman who had accumulated 21,000 hours in the cockpit during her fifty years of flying. I read that she was still an active pilot, training and flight testing students for the Peterborough Flying Club and Trent Air. This was a story for me.

I met Marion Orr at the Flying Club in late April of that year. We talked, then I flew with her, capturing this incredible woman on videotape. Marion was born in Toronto on the 25th of June 1918. Orphaned at an early age, she started working full-time after completing grade eight. Her ambition was to fly. By 1940 she'd earned her private pilot's licence. A year later she'd earned her commercial licence. In 1942, the year I was born, she was hired as manager and chief flying instructor at the St. Catharine's Flying Club, the first woman in Canada to operate a flying club. In 1943, she went to England with British Overseas Airways. She worked as a pilot with the Air Transport Auxiliary. Marion flew aircraft from factories to bases throughout the United Kingdom and delivered Tiger Moths, Hurricanes, and Spitfires. In between, she delivered Harvards, Miles Masters, Oxfords, and Mosquitoes, but it was the Spitfire that remained her favourite.

At the end of the war, Marion returned to Canada where she was employed as a flying instructor with Gillies Flying Service at Buttonville Airport just to the north of Toronto. By 1956 she moved a few miles northwest of Buttonville to Maple. Here she became the first woman in Canada to operate an airport. In the 1980s, the Maple airstrip was bulldozed by developers to build houses.

In 1961 she'd earned her instructor's rating on the rotor-wing helicopter. That year an engine failed sending the chopper crashing to the ground, breaking Marion's back. "It was my only serious accident," she told me. "I had some scary landings in Britain during the war, but I never seriously damaged any aircraft," she said.

One of the highlights in her life was flying with the Canadian forces in 1983. She flew as a passenger with the Snowbirds aerobatic team. Marion has been initiated into the Forest of Friendship, a memorial to the late Amelia Earhart. She's also a member of Canada's Aviation Hall of Fame in Edmonton, Alberta. A lot of her former students have gone on to work for various airlines, some flying 747s and others becoming flying instructors. In October of 1993, Marion Orr was made a Member of the Order of Canada.

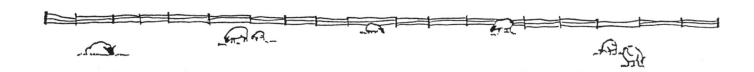

Fifteenth annual perfect pie contest judges hard at work picking the best
pie in each category in Warkworth, Ontario

THE PERFECT PIE

When it comes to dessert, my favourite has to be pie. Cakes and squares are okay, but they don't really hold a candle, as far as I'm concerned, to a slice of good olde-fashioned apple pie with a wedge of cheddar cheese. And now my favourite pie has gone one step further towards perfection, because my wife Donna has added pears to her recipe.

This brings me to a story of a perfect-pie competition. It was on the 5th of November 1994 that I journeyed across country from my Markham area home to the pretty Northumberland County village of Warkworth. I was going to that eastern Ontario community to cover the fifteenth Annual Perfect Pie Contest. I'd read about it the year before in the Sunday edition of the *Toronto Star*. As I drove east on that damp and misty fall morning, I passed through the hamlet of Whitevale, then across the top of Whitby, Ajax, and Oshawa. My constant companion as I travel the highways and byways of this province is CBC Radio, and the weekend program *Fresh Air* was in progress. Host Tom Allen was doing a live interview over the phone with some of the pie contest's organizers and participants. One of his interviews was Norma McCleary, a lifelong resident of Warkworth, and winner of several Perfect Pie titles. Norma was the first person I had contacted about doing a story a couple months earlier, and she had consented to talk on camera to me that day.

Created by a man, it was originally called the Northumberland Perfect Pie Contest. Graham Woods thought up the idea as a fund-raising project for the Warkworth Improvement Committee back in 1980. It was only open to residents of the county at that time. The late Edna Thompson was the one to suggest it be held in November, because she thought it would make a wonderful show on a dull November day. She was certainly right as far as the weather was concerned this day. The Warkworth Chapter of the Order of the Eastern Star took over sponsorship in 1990 and the name was changed to the Perfect Pie Contest. It's now open to everyone, no matter where you live.

A fact that I wasn't aware of was that most of the bakers make their pies that very morning. I asked Norma McCleary on camera what makes the perfect pie? "You have to get up early in the morning and it has to be made fresh," she said. "I make mine on a marble slab with lard, flour, and water and bake it as soon as possible, and eat it even sooner."

I shot the interview with Norma at her home. When I finished, Norma invited me to stay for soup and a sandwich with her family. I had to turn this wonderful offer down because I still had to take pictures of the village and the judges searching for that perfect pie. Before I left Norma's cozy home, she informed me that she'd entered five pies and that her two daughters had entered as well. Then, with a big smile on her face, she told me her three granddaughters had entered the competition for the first time. Norma's so proud of winning the perfect pie title in the past that she displays it on her personalized licence plate. The plates on her car read MY PIE 1.

When the competitors deliver their creations to the town hall, their pies are entered anonymously. The judges have no idea who made them. A team of five judges and a co-ordinator spend the better part of three hours tasting their way through dozens of pies. There were ninety entries in 1994. The judges take this job seriously as they look at the pies for eye appeal, consistancy of filling, and, of course, taste. They'll judge fruit and filled pies. There's savoury and chocolate pies. Each judge will probably taste as many as

Photograph courtesy of Norma McCleary

Norma McCleary takes home the trophy for 'best filled pie' in 1986. The award was presented to Norma, on the left, by the late Edna Thompson and Donna McDonald, the Warkworth Fair Queen.

fifty different pies before they're finished. This contest has been referred to as the world series of pie making.

Finally, the winning pies are taken up onto the stage. They're set on tables in front of the appropriate trophies. At 1:30 p.m., the doors were opened to the public and Leslie Campbell, Norma McCleary's schoolteacher daughter began tinkling the ivories on an upright piano. Within seconds, Leslie was joined by a drummer and guitar player and the familiar tune of "Sweet Georgia Brown" filled the hall. For a four-dollar admission fee, you receive a piece of the non-winning pie and a cup of coffee or tea. During this

time, I met a couple of media colleagues for the first time: Mark Hoult, editor of the *Warkworth Journal* and Dave Lockwood, owner/manager of radio station CKOL in Campbellford. They'd come to cover the event as well. I ended up being interviewed on radio by Dave, a first for me.

Then the moment everyone was waiting for arrived. It was time to announce the winners of the various catagories and here are just a few of them. Eric Lorenzen of Marmora took the men's open, with his pear pie. Our Norma took first place for her sour cream lemon in the filled category, and first place for eye appeal with her burnt sugar. Jean Peters, the Past Matron of the Order of the Eastern Star called to the stage eight-year-old Lauren Weaver. She took first prize for twelve and under. Then Jean went on to announce the two honourable mentions for twelve and under and, surprise, surprise, they just happened to be Lauren's sisters Katie and Charlotte.

They're the three granddaughters of Norma McCleary.

Now for the winner of the Perfect Pie title . . . it's Velma Harper of Roseneath. She won it for her delicious-looking and obviously great-tasting key-lime pie. In '92, Velma won Best Fruit and in '93 she won Best Senior. As the contest drew to a close, the winning pies were auctioned off with the proceeds going to local charities. The auctioneer was Rod Williams whose father and grandfather were both auctioneers; Norma McCleary is his mother-in-law. By golly she's a popular woman in these parts. In the fifteen years of competition, 1305 pies have been judged. In 1989, Judy May's Moose Savoury pie brought a record five hundred and fifty dollars at the auction. The organizers feel that this had to be the most expensive pie in the world, worthy of a mention in *The Guinness Book of Records.*

Believe it or not, for some reason I missed out on tasting a piece of those magnificent-looking pies. I phoned home as I was leaving Warkworth to tell my wife when to expect me, and that I hadn't sampled a piece of pie. When I walked through the door at home that night Donna had cut me a large slice of apple-pear pie, accompanied by a wedge of cheddar cheese. What a great day it had been.

THERE'S REALLY NO BAD BEER, JUST BETTER BEER

I first heard about Ian Bowering when I was at the Lang Pioneer Village north of Keene in the Peterborough area. I was standing next to a cider press and the aroma coming from it reminded me of my passion and hobby: beer. The museum's assistant curator, Dorette Carter, told me that I must meet one of Canada's most knowledgeable people on the subject, and proceeded to tell me about Ian.

Ian Bowering is the curator of Inverarden Regency Cottage Museum in Cornwall. The house was built for retired North-west Company fur trader John McDonald in 1816. Restored by Parks Canada, it's now operated by the Stormont, Dundas and Glengarry Historical Society.

Curator Bowering is a professional historian with a master's degree in museology and history from the University of Toronto. As a child, he and his family came by passenger liner from England to Canada. During that crossing, young Master Ian swiped a church key, more commonly known as a bottle opener, from the ship as it journeyed the Atlantic. He feels that this could have something to do with the other facet of his life, his fascination with beer. "As a student," Ian said, "I was more or less a failure. In fact, I wouldn't have got very far at all if it hadn't been for history. When I read about Ontario's glorious Loyalist past, I discovered that the United Empire Loyalists brought their tradition of beer making with them. After learning that the Loyalists actually enjoyed their beer, I had to discover what that beer must have tasted like. My father, being English, thought the drinking age of twenty-one in Ontario was odd, so we made beer at home. We both came to the conclusion that beer and history do, in fact, go together."

So with this knowledge, Ian wrote his university thesis which would later become his first book, *The Art and Mystery of Brewing in Ontario*. Two years later his second book was published, *In Search of the Perfect Brew*. Then in March of '94 his third beer book came off the press. This one was titled, *In Search of the Perfect Brew . . . the Saga Continues*. All three were published by General Store Publishing House in Burnstown, Ontario.

Ian is also a recognized beer taster. Oh gosh, what a cross he has to bear. He frequently gives talks on his favourite subject and claims: "There are really no bad beers . . . just better beers." When he's been on the lecture circuit, I've attended three of his talks and found them extremely educational with loads of humour thrown in. "My first enjoyable experience with a cold, refreshing bottle of beer," said Ian, "took place during a spring high school field trip. My friends and I happened upon a couple of fishermen willing to sell us a six pack of Molson Golden to further our studies. I had tried beer before, but never enjoyed it as much as I did that day. We sat under a tree in a pasture, while the rest of the class was investigating various forms of natural history."

When I was doing my story at Inverarden, Ian invited three of his friends to participate in a beertasting. They included David Anderson, tenant of Bethune-Thompson House in the historic village of Williamstown, William Baker, a Montreal collector of Canadian historical artifacts, and David Tuck, a publican from nearby Williamstown. None of these men had been at a tasting before. Ian stresses to individuals and groups that appreciation and not over-indulgence is the key to the art of enjoying beer. The brewing of beer in North America over the past decade and a half has vastly improved, and I feel most of the credit should go to the micro-breweries. Brewing non-preserv-

Drawing by John Izod

The Feathers Pub was included in Ian Bowering's book: *In Search of the Perfect Brew... the Saga Continues*. The Feathers, in which I'm a partner, is located at 962 Kingston Road in Toronto.

ative products, with flavours for almost everyone's palate, has changed the beer market forever. The addition of brew-pubs and U-brews gives the true connoisseur a reason to jump for joy. In fact, the major breweries are finally sitting up and taking notice that we expect more in taste and quality than they had been providing. Even at The Feathers, the British-style pub in Toronto in which I'm a partner, Ian Innes, chief partner and general manager, has swung over to many micro-brewery beers. The only Labatt and Molson beer that's available is by the bottle. The sixteen draught lines are now either import, micro or our own beer. Simon Cowe of Lakeside Brewery and Wine, a few blocks east of us on Kingston Road, delivers wort to our specially-built brew room, where the yeast is added. After fermentation, the beer is filtered, kegged, and carbonated. Our own line of Beaches Best Bitter has been a tremendous hit with the regulars.

When Ian Bowering launched his third beer book, he did it from the Granite Brewery at the corner of Mount Pleasant and Eglinton Avenue in Toronto. With an invitation from Ron Keefe, the brewer and proprieter, Ian held court that cold winter's evening, standing next to a fireplace in the brew-pub's cozy dining room. He told the audience that, to do his research, he'd travelled throughout Ontario and Quebec visiting micro-breweries and brew-pubs. He'd held tastings with fellow beer enthusiasts, comparing lager to lager, ale to ale, and stout to stout. Tim Gordon, publisher of General Store Publishing House, asked him to keep the book to 165 pages, but after collecting so much material, Ian ended up with a 250-page book.

By the way, Ian doesn't just do beer books. In 1993, he and five members of the Tri-County Writer's Guild compiled a guide book for day-trippers interested in travelling throughout the United Empire Loyalist Counties of Eastern Ontario. It's a book with seven-day trips through Stormont, Dundas and Glengarry called *Bowering's Guide to Eastern Ontario*.

What can we expect in the future from curator/author Bowering? He's designing a working brewery for Upper Canada Village near Morrisburg. It will be a replica of an old brewery where the visitor will be able to enjoy a beer made the same way that the pioneers brewed theirs. Ian's also writing a book on the history of armouries in Ontario and is co-writing a book with his artist wife Lor Pelton and his brother-in-law called *365 Reasons Why to Take the Day Off . . . the Canadian Edition*.

THE GINGER PRESS

I dropped into Owen Sound's Economic Development and Tourism office one day, looking for story ideas. Mary Price, an officer with the department, suggested that I stop by the Ginger Press and say hello to publisher Maryann Hogbin. On Second Avenue East, in the heart of Owen Sound's business district, the building looked like an old-fashioned bookstore. The front window displays were being changed for the Christmas season. The store itself was a bookstore, but it's more than that because the publisher has found a niche in helping local writers get their words into print through self-publishing. Maryann Hogbin started her business as a mail-order bookstore in the hamlet of Kilsyth; then, in 1984, she moved it to Owen Sound. Three years later, she'd become a publisher giving a voice to the community through her books. By the time I'd discovered Maryann, she'd published thirteen books and two magazines. *Sounding* is a quarterly, providing an outlet for local artists and writers. *The Owen Sounder* provides a link between local residents and the business community. In 1994, Maryann published the story of *Beautiful Joe*. Written by Margaret Marshall Saunders, the 304-page book is based on the true story of a dog in Meaford, Ontario. After an 1895 edition was found, the Ginger Press reproduced it, commemorating the 100th anniversary of the original Canadian publication.

"There are two kinds of publishing going on right now in Canada," said Maryann. "One is conventional publishing, and we're seeing fewer Canadian authors having their books brought into print, and the other is the growing market of self-publishing. This is where people who have a message are doing the publishing process themselves." A couple of self-publishing authors were at Ginger Press that morning. Rachel Oliver has a love for cartooning and a passion for horses, so she produced a book called *Life Around The Track.* Edward Myatt teaches knitting part-time and his book, *The Hand-knitted Christmas Stocking Book* was into its second printing.

Also visiting that morning was Andrew Armitage, an author and director of the Owen Sound Library. "This bookstore doubles as an information centre, as an informal education centre, as a gathering place for people in town. At the same time it publishes books by and about Owen Sounders and this area," said Andrew. "It's a beehive of activity and one of the most unusual bookstores as a librarian that I've ever been in." Andrew has been writing books and radio scripts about this area of the province for over twenty years. Maryann asked him to write a book on the Bruce Peninsula. Six months later, Andrew and the production team at the Press had the *Bruce Peninsula Explorer* on the store shelf. Andrew's book was illustrated by Catherine Caple who has been designing and illustrating books and magazines for the Ginger Press from the beginning. Catherine is not only a professional graphic artist she's a jazz singer as well.

As I was packing up to leave, I met writer/poet Susan Gibson. She put together a hand-bound, numbered edition book about Agnes Macphail, the first woman elected to the Parliament in Ottawa.

It's titled *Agnes Macphail: Letters from the Commons.* Susan told me that it was Maryann's prompting that made her do the book.

"The Ginger Press is known by many as the social and intellectual centre of Grey-Bruce Counties," said Susan. It's not uncommon on any given day to find writers and artists in the store just chatting with the proprietor. Maryann and her husband Stephen chose Owen Sound as a good community to raise their two daughters. Despite all the dire predictions about the book industry in Canada, regional publishing is alive and well at the Ginger Press.

IN RETROSPECT

$2

INSURANCE &
INVESTMENT PLANNING
Ottawa, Ontario
Tel. (613) 728-0137

JANUARY 1994   VOL. 1 NO. 4   The Best of Yesterday's News   DISPLAY UNTIL JAN. 31

DOUGLAS THINKS TORIES DYING

December 24, 1973

OTTAWA (CP)

Former NDP leader Tommy Douglas predicts the Conservative party will disappear as Canada moves towards a two-party political system.

Douglas, interviewed for a television program, said the New Democratic Party is rapidly becoming one of the major parties in the country.

"The Conservatives, who have less lasting grass roots, are more likely to fade out of the scene. In the final analysis we will see in Canada a Liberal party absorbing Conservatives and becoming the party of the right against the New Democrats."

"I don't think there is going to be an immediate fading away, but I think inevitably we'll move toward a two-party system.

"I don't think the Social Credit party is going to be a major factor and I certainly don't think the Waffle will be a major factor."

Douglas said he does not believe Prime Minister Pierre Elliot Trudeau is a socialist. "Certainly in economic terms he's a right-winger."

He said a formal coalition of Liberals and Conservatives is more likely than a coalition of Liberals and New Democrats.

"When it comes to curbing the power of the vested interests in this country they (the Liberals) are going to be very wary and they're going to be very reluctant.

IN RETROSPECT

15,000 circulation

INSURANCE &
INVESTMENT PLANNING
Ottawa, Ontario
Tel. (613) 728-0137

APRIL 1994 VOL. 1 NO. 5   The Best of Yesterday's News   KANATA, ONTARIO Edition

EMPRESS OF IRELAND GOES DOWN

May 29, 1914

37 SURVIVORS OF 1422 SOULS

EXTRA!

NEARLY NAKED IN THE WATER, FROST IN THE AIR, THEY DIED OF EXPOSURE

Twenty-Two Succumbed - Of the 350 Landed at Rimouski Only 12 Were Women- Mr. and Mrs. Black of Ottawa Tell First Brief Story of the Tragedy

1,030 ARE MISSING OR LOST AND ONLY 117 ARE KNOWN TO BE SAFE

(CP) - The Crippled Collier and the

IN RETROSPECT

During the two years that reporter John Darby filled in as assignment editor in our newsroom, he periodically placed story ideas in my mail-slot. The press release announcing the launch of *In Retrospect*, a new national publication, is an example.

In Retrospect, the Best of Yesterday's News, is a unique monthly publication. The Ottawa paper, a nostalgia newspaper mainly for secondary school students, first appeared in 1993. Jim Boone, the creator and the paper's editor, hopes that yesterday's news will be a drawing card and a valuable history lesson. Born in Nova Scotia, Jim's a graduate of Humber College in Toronto where he majored in public relations. The idea for the paper came to him when his wife was tidying up their apartment and asked Jim to throw out an old box of newspapers. He was astonished to find out how much he enjoyed reading some of the antique articles.

Many of the stories reprinted in the paper were found at the National Library and Archives of Canada. The building contains a wealth of material on microfilm from every decade of the twentieth century. Jim also discovers items from the 1700s and 1800s. Here's an example: "January 1963, Manning Son Wants Politics." It tells of a young Preston Manning wanting to follow in his father's footsteps in a political career. There is a story from July 1940, where an unarmed woman captures a German pilot. Then there's this one from December 1973: "I'm Very Rich, Trudeau Admits." Finally, this news story from June 30th, 1947. "Flying Saucer Streaks Across Ottawa Valley."

"Currently over ten thousand high school students across Canada are enjoying *In Retrospect*," said Jim, "and I'm hoping that these students will take the free paper home, so that the entire family can enjoy it." The paper is worked on in various locations. I met Jim, the morning I did the story, at the home of Mark McNab, the circulation manager and one of a team of six part-time employees. Mark works with a computer and phone from his basement. Jim puts full-time hours into his paper, but so far it doesn't pay the rent. He also works as a public relations consultant and general manager for the Ottawa-Hull Blues Festival.

After we'd finished shooting the story on a glorious warm September day, I invited Jim for a beer. As a visitor to Ottawa, I was able to introduce him to a pub down in the Byward Market. He'd never been in The Heart and Crown on Clarence Street. It's a comfortable pub and has become my favourite dining spot. It's an Irish pub where you can be sure the two characters running the bar, Pedro and Dennis, will keep you entertained. After this well-deserved break, I bid farewell to Jim Boone and headed up to Parliament Hill to do my on-camera. My wife Donna and I lived in Ottawa in the early eighties and it brought back memories of the hundreds of times Luigi Della Penta and I lugged our television gear up the hill from Global's office in the National Press Building. Returning to do the ending to my own story, who did I spot as I drove up to the top? None other than my old friend Luigi. When I first worked with him, he was fresh from college and we were teamed as cameraman and soundman. Luigi later became a cameraman so, when he saw me, he offered to shoot the closer for me. I was delighted, because 99.9 percent of the time, I position myself in front of the camera and it often takes a few tries to get the proper framing. Luigi called out: "Hey Terry, I'm rolling." Looking into the camera lens I said: "As a nationalist, Jim Boone wants to publish his paper in French as well, so that high school students all across Canada can read it. I'm Terry Culbert for Global News in Ottawa, Ontario."

Photograph: Colleen Maguire/Goderich

Author Beulah Homan at her typewriter. Her home overlooks
the Maitland River in Goderich.

THE RIDGE TRILOGY

In January of '92, I was in Clinton doing a story on Cyril Leeper, an incredible portrait painter. Entering his studio gave me the feeling of being with a European artist a couple of hundred years ago. Cyril was putting the finishing touches on a portrait of Dr. Mario Cauchi, a highly respected general practitioner in Huron County who had come over from Goderich for his final sitting. When I'd completed my story, Mrs.Leeper invited Dr. Cauchi and me to join them for lunch. As we sat in the dining room, Dr. Cauchi told me about Beulah Homan, a Goderich author.

A month later, I was pulling up the laneway of her home. Mrs. Homan and her late husband Ben built their house overlooking the Maitland River, just inland from Lake Huron. I was greeted at the door by an elegant woman and her poodle, named Pierre. Mrs. Homan was dressed in a pretty green-satin pant-suit, her thick silver hair combed back into a ballet-bun. "I was born in Ashfield Township eighty-two years ago," she said. "When I was a child growing up on the shores of Lake Huron, my father decided to move our family from the country, where we attended a one-room school house, into the town of Goderich. The schools were larger there, and he thought that we'd get a better education. When I was in grade four, I wrote a short article on interior decorating. I decided to send it to the *Family Herald* and *Weekly Star* in Montreal. To my amazement, they sent me a cheque for four dollars."

It would be seventy years before she'd sit down and take up writing seriously. She'd always been fascinated with Canadian and local history, and in 1989, her first historical novel *A Place Called the Ridge* was published. Two years later, a sequel entitled *Daybreak at the Ridge* was released. Her first book begins in 1839 with the arrival in Upper Canada from England of the two wealthy Sandy brothers and their families. Although the characters are fictional, Mrs. Homan used her family to illustrate the people in the story. Gilbert Sandy is portrayed in the book by a photograph of her father. The twin Kingsley sisters, Mary Jane and Em, are illustrated with photographs of Mrs. Homan herself as a child. The third book *Summer at the Ridge* completes the Sandy trilogy. The richly detailed, historical novels have received an enthusiastic response from readers across North America and Britain. They're published by Natural Heritage/Natural History Inc. of Toronto.

The Great Meadow and Ridgewood Farm, where Mrs. Homan lived for nearly twenty-five years, was chosen as the backdrop for her novels. Today the old country home called The Ridge is owned and occupied by Mrs. Homan's son Keith and her daughter in-law Joanne. "My friends told me that I should write about something I'm familiar with," she told me, "so that's why I chose this area." The only other book that Mrs. Homan has had published was a childrens book titled *Chadwick the Chipmunk and the Sunflower Seeds.*

When we'd finished doing the story, Mrs. Homan disappeared, returning moments later with a tray filled with scrumptous-looking goodies, sandwiches, along with an assortment of fruit and cookies. As we chatted over lunch, I told her that I would be staying in Clinton overnight as I was doing a story on a family bakery the following day. Preparing to leave, Mrs. Homan gave me a bag full of food. She was worried that a big lad like me may become weak from hunger later that afternoon.

Photograph courtesy of Ontario Archives Ref: S4748

Oil springs, 1867. First oil strike in North America was here ten years earlier.

OIL SPRINGS: WHERE THE OIL INDUSTRY BEGAN

Every summer from the age of eight to sixteen, I visited my aunt Marjorie and uncle Ches Patrick for a week in Froomfield, a tiny hamlet on the St. Clair River between Sarnia and Corunna. At that time my uncle and aunt shared a big house with her mother and her brother Field Simpson. The city of Sarnia and the twenty miles along the St. Clair shoreline was called "chemical valley." Uncle Ches worked for Dow Chemical, Aunt Marj for Polymar, and Field was with Imperial Oil. Almost every day, after Field came home from work, we'd head out onto the river in his motorboat. And always by Field's side was his cocker spaniel Brownie. We would cruise alongside the enormous Great Lake freighters, often waving to a deckhand waving to us from far above. Now that I think of it, the deckhand was probably warning us not to get so close. At night, the horizon looked like a fairyland, with thousands of lights and flames burning from the top of the stacks.

Most people are probably unaware that the first oil field in North America was just a few miles from Sarnia itself. The Lambton County village of Oil Springs is Canada's oil heritage district. Hope Morritt, a journalist, novelist and poet, wrote a book about the early pioneers who discovered liquid gold in the fields of Oil Springs and Petrolia. Published by Quarry Press, she titled it *Rivers of Oil*. Hope moved to Sarnia from Edmonton with her husband in the 1960s, and was surprised to learn that Canada's petroleum industry began in Ontario. "I grew up in western Canada and I thought that the oil industry began in Alberta," she told me.

Hope and I met one morning in Oil Springs. We drove over the muddy roads of the Fairbank oil fields looking for Charles Oliver Fairbank. We finally spotted him hard at work on top of a holding tank. I shot a few scenes of Charles and Hope walking and talking to each other. Charles is owner-operator of Charles Fairbank Oil Properties Limited, which he claims is the only oil business in the world that has been operated continuously by the same family. The Fairbanks started it in 1861. Charles pumps four hundred wells today on part of the original two-square-mile bust and boom land. His great-grandfather, John Henry Fairbank, devised the ingenious, cost-effective method of running numerous wells from one power source through the use of jerker lines. An estimated ten million barrels of oil came from the small field we were standing on during an eight-year period in the 1850s.

In her book, Hope dispels the myth that the Americans were the first to discover oil in North America. The Americans have been telling the world for years that Colonel Edwin L. Drake discovered oil at Titusville, Pennsylvania in 1859. However, they have ignored the fact that James Miller Williams discovered oil in southwestern Ontario in 1857. Williams was refining and selling his oil by the summer of 1858, a year before America's Drake sank his first drill bit.

This is a wonderful and well-organized area for tourists. There's a well-marked Oil Heritage District self-guided tour that visitors can do in their own cars. Petrolia Discovery is a nineteenth century public oil field with sixteen producing wells. Right next door to Fairbank's, in Oil Springs, is the Oil Museum of Canada. Museum manager Donna McGuire and her staff have set up fascinating exhibits showing how oil was formed under the earth's crust, how it was prospected for, then drilled and extracted. Tours are offered all year long.

ONTARIO PLACE NAMES

Before Mike Farmer moved to the technical area, called playback, he was a co-ordinator on Global's *News at Noon*, producer Larry Jackson's right-hand man. A lot of his time was spent finding guests to appear on the daily noon-hour show. Each day, magazines and just-released books would cross his desk in the hopes that their authors would receive some exposure. One such book came in called *Ontario Place Names* by David E. Scott. He had compiled a book of historical, offbeat and humourous origins of the names of close to one thousand communities in our province. Mike gave it to me because it had been turned down at the *News at Noon* meeting. I noticed the publisher was Whitecap Books of Vancouver, but the author lived in southwestern Ontario. It turned out that David lived in Ailsa Craig, just a few miles from my hometown of Lucan. I gave David a call and set up a date to do the story.

Ailsa Craig is forty minutes northwest of London. David's office is on the second floor of the W. G. Thompson Seed Company. When I arrived, I found him sitting at his computer puffing on a pipe. Casually dressed in a sweat shirt and jeans, he turned and welcomed me to Ailsa Craig. Over his thirty-odd year career, he's been a police reporter for the *North Bay Nugget*, bureau chief for Canadian Press in both Toronto and Windsor, and travel editor for the *London Free Press*. He held that post for nearly fifteen years. David has travelled in more than one hundred countries throughout the world and, as a full-time writer/photographer, he's written ten books. At the time of my visit, he was working on humourous fiction. "Let's shatter the myth that writers are wealthy people," he said. "I couldn't even pay the rent on this office if it weren't for my very long-suffering wife, God bless her." To help pay the bills, he runs a custom wordmanship and public relations firm called "Rent-A-Writer."

The reason David wrote *Ontario Place Names* was that he felt most people know something about their local history, but they're probably not aware of the stories and origins behind their own village or town. For a community to make it into his book, it must have a population of at least two hundred. *Ontario Place Names* is a concise, factual chronicle of events leading to the naming of these communities and a valuable addition to the library of anyone with a passion for regional history.

David was like the old reporters that I remember from my late teens and early twenties; he looked like the hard-bitten newspaper man that seemed to be the norm when I first began my career. As I made my departure, he invited me to return. "Come back anytime, summertime is excellent. We play croquet in our front garden."

To illustrate my two-minute feature, I went to four villages. I started with the Huron County village of Zurich, probably best known today for its Bean Festival, which is held on the fourth Saturday of August every year. Although most of the early settlers were German, the founder was Swiss. Frederick K. Knell decided in 1854 to name the community Zurich after the city in Switzerland.

Then I showed Ailsa Craig. The Middlesex County village was settled in 1835 by David Craig. He donated land for the first railway station on the condition it be named Craig's Station. It turned out that another place of that name existed, so the settlement was named Ailsa Craig after a huge rock which protrudes from the water on the west coast of Scotland. The third place I photographed was the Waterloo County village of New Dundee. Scotsman John Miller settled this area and called it Bonnie New Dundee after a city on the Firth of Tay in Scotland. When the post office was established in 1852, the village fathers dropped the "Bonnie." Finally, I chose the village of Kirkton because it had just made it into David's book, having a population of 204. Situated a few miles to the southwest of Stratford, it was here that Timothy Eaton opened one of his first two stores. The other was in nearby St. Marys. That was in the 1860s, the beginning of the Eaton department store empire.

I ended my story with a little personal trivia. I put a microphone on and, looking into the camera, I told a story that wasn't in *Ontario Place Names*. When I was eight years old, I came from Lucan to sing in a contest at the Kirkton community hall. This was the preliminary to a much larger event, the Kirkton Garden Party. For some reason, I won the semi-final. Months later I returned to sing in the finals at the Kirkton Garden Party, a very big annual event in these parts. As hundreds of people sat in front of the open-air bandshell, it was time for me to go on. I could be the next Tom Jones! When I stood alone up there looking down at all those faces, I was terrified. My knees knocked, my lips trembled and cold sweat trickled down my back. I was there all alone except for Mrs. Muriel Cobleigh, my music teacher. She was playing the piano. Well, I froze and my singing career ended right then and there, in the village of Kirkton.

Madeleine McCabe's late mother, May Greenshaw, at the doorway of her Knaresborough, North Yorkshire home. When I snapped this photograph in April of '92, Mrs. Greenshaw was writing to Madeleine and her son-in-law John.

THE CHICKEN COOP COUNTRY BAKERY

For more than a quarter of a century, John and Madeleine McCabe have been creating delectable tidbits at their Chicken Coop Bakery in the hamlet of Greenbank, a few miles north of Whitby. When they first arrived from England in 1962, they weren't bakers, they were newlyweds who had left their family and friends behind in Knaresborough, North Yorkshire, to start a new life together in Toronto. John was a corporate management accountant and Madeleine worked as a secretary. But, by 1968, John was developing stomach ulcers and was advised by his doctor to get into a less stressful occupation. In Greenbank they found and purchased a chicken farm, complete with three thousand chickens and a gas bar. Not long after they'd taken over the operation the bottom fell out of the chicken market; it was not the prescription John's doctor intended.

Just at this time, Madeleine's mother flew over from Yorkshire to see how they were making out as chicken farmers. Shortly after Mrs. Greenshaw arrived, she came up with a solution to their problem. "Why don't you open a bakeshop," she said, "I can't get a decent loaf of bread anywhere around here." Being a good cook and an enthusiastic baker herself, Madeleine's mother wrote down dozens of her own recipes that she had stored away in her head. Word soon spread throughout the countryside and customers began lining up each morning for their fresh bread. The McCabes now produce thirty different kinds. They've got bread representing every area of Canada. They also bake traditional soda bread and Yorkshire teacake.

As the business grew, the McCabes needed additional staff. Donna and Michele Oldnall, twin sisters, lived close by. They started working at the bakery part-time while still in high school. Today, with their schooling completed, these lovely ladies work full-time. Sheila Williamson has been with them forever. If you're ever in need of cheering up, just follow Sheila around the bakery for a few minutes. The McCabes have three grown children; Michael, Michelle and James. Michael has joined the Chicken Coop team.

For many years John drove to Toronto every Saturday at four in the morning, taking a vanload of baked goods to the St. Lawrence Farmers Market. While he was on the road, Madeleine was down in their spacious kitchen baking for the early morning customers. They make their own line of Scottish Bannock and Irish soda bread mixes to bake at home. They even sell their own jams and chutney. My favourite item from the bakery is their Eccles cake. Made with unbleached white flour and filled with currants and raisins, two hundred and eighty scrumptious cakes are baked in the oven. Next to the Eccles cakes made by my daughters' grandmother Cicely Veighey, they're the best I've ever tasted. The cakes were named after the northern English town of Eccles, near Manchester. An Eccles cake and a good hot mug of tea is one of my favourite little pleasures in life.

I did my story with John and Madeleine in March of '91. Since then, my wife Donna, a fantastic cook and dessert maker in her own right, has made friends with this wonderful couple. The following year I was in Scotland and England on holidays, and stopped to pay Mrs. Greenshaw a visit at her retirement cottage in Knaresborough. When she opened the door, she was holding a pen and an air mail letter addressed to Madeleine and John. I captured that moment on film and that's the photograph accompanying this story. A large colour blowup hangs on the wall of the Chicken Coop Bakery. Sadly, Mrs. Greenshaw passed away October 28th, 1993. She was an inspiration for all.

I took this photograph in Wetherby, West
Yorkshire, England in April of '92. Jo Lister's shop
in Acton, Ontario was named after her hometown.

A BIT OF YORKSHIRE

When I was in Acton doing a story on a family-run flour mill, I spotted an old home on one of the sidestreets that had been converted into a British shop called "'Wetherby's." Being a lover of anything from the old country, I popped in. Immediately, I fell in love with the place, which reminded me of my many trips abroad.

I returned a few weeks later to do a story. "We came to Canada twenty-eight years ago," said Jo Lister, the shop owner. "We left England on the 15th of January 1964. I mean, it couldn't have been a worse time of year to come by sea." The Lister family, including their three small children, had left Wetherby, a small market town in Yorkshire, not far from Harrogate and the walled city of York. Her husband Wayne fortunately had a job waiting for him on this side of the Atlantic. The family survived their first harsh Canadian winter, through the following spring, summer and fall in their newly adopted country. Then winter number two rolled around. "Everything began to look a lot better until Christmas time," said Jo. "Then every time I heard the radio play, 'I'll be home for Christmas,' I'd burst into tears." Missing the British way of life was the driving force behind Jo's decision to open up her shop. She named it after her home town of Wetherby.

There's a room filled with children's books and toys, like Enid Blyton's Noddy. There's Rupert and Paddington bears and toys and tapes of Thomas the Tank Engine. The food room is extremely popular with its teas, jams, and jellies. I saw treacle, and one package contained enough ingredients to make up six pounds of Seville marmalade. There's a savory snack called Twiglets, with Marmite baked on the outside. They're just the thing to munch on when you're watching Coronation Street. By the way, you can now shop in person or by mail at Wetherby's Coronation Street Corner Shop for your collectibles as authorized by the North-American distributors of the official magazine of Coronation Street.

"For a lot of people who come in," said Jo, "it's a real nostalgia trip. They see things that they knew and had when they were children. It's interesting to hear many of them say as they leave, 'Oh my grandmother used to send me those. Every Christmas we used to get a selection box.' So the store really does bring back happy memories to a lot of them."

When I was doing my story, I met Mary Kerr and her granddaughter Alison. Mary and her husband came to Canada from Surrey in 1946, just after the war. She's shopped at Wetherby's a number of times and it always brings back warm memories. Another guest arrived that morning; Eldor Otis, a colleague and graphic artist from Global, just happened to be in the neighbourhood and spotted the news wagon. Wearing his tweed cap, he looked very much the country squire out shopping, so I used him in a couple of scenes.

The front parlour of the old house is filled with china and figurines. Jo tries to stock her store with items from Yorkshire whenever possible. When I was there, she had wonderful prints of the Yorkshire Dales, painted by Yorkshireman Alan Ingham. They depicted farmers with their trusted border collies, tending their sheep.

Jo keeps a visitors' book at the front counter for customer comments. This is a sample from it:

Takes me back to my childhood.
Felt like being in England.
Great memories of home.

It really is a wonderful store. If you can't manage a trip back to the old country, I highly recommend a visit to Jo Lister's "Wetherby's" in Acton.

Sipping a pint at the Rovers Return. My friend Doug McLellan, a Wallaceburg native, with Marilyn and Neil Malcolm. I'm the one in between the publicans.

Photograph: Sam Kinsmen/Wallaceburg News

ROVERS RETURN

I was driving from Sarnia to Chatham after completing my story on Canada's only breeder of hairless cats. It was a late winter's afternoon as I headed for my sister Dana's home where I was going to stay the night so that we could have a short visit together. As I approached the outskirts of Wallace-burg I spotted a familiar name on the outside of a building. The Rovers Return Inn is probably the most famous pub name in the world, famous because it is the centre of life on Britain's longest running television drama-series, *Coronation Street*. It went to air December 9th, 1960. Three times a week, millions of people all over the world watch this show. It's the continuing story of people living in a working-class neighbourhood in the north of England. Their lives all have a common thread: their neighbourhood pub. Granada Television produces the show in Manchester. I've been to their studios; it's well worth a visit if you're in the area.

With my love for pubs and a pint of good dark beer, I decided to pull into Wallaceburg's Rovers. Once inside, a jar of Smithwicks in hand, the world seemed a much better place. I called my sister to see if she'd join me for dinner here rather than in Chatham. As she is somewhat like her older brother, the idea sounded terrific to her. After Dana arrived, I introduced her to the publicans Marilyn and Neil Malcolm. They introduced us to some of their regulars and then we dined on Marilyn's fabulous fish and chips. It was a wonderful evening, and I told them I'd like to return one day to do a story. Within a couple of months I was back. Accompanying me was my friend Doug McLellan who was born and raised in Wallace-burg.

Marilyn and Neil Malcolm came to Canada from Leeds to start a new life with their children. She wanted to open a fish and chip shop and he wanted a pub. They both ended up getting what they wanted. "The reason Neil and I decided to call our pub the Rovers Return," said Marilyn, "is because *Coronation Street* is my favourite television show. It really reminds me of home." Neil added: "It's turned into a full-fledged British pub, including all the gossip. Marilyn loves to hear gossip." Marilyn's family in England own nine fish and chip shops in Leeds. They send her little packets of their secret batter ingredients across the Atlantic. Take it from me, the Rovers' fish and chips are excellent.

Thirty-five percent of the pub's regulars are transplanted English, Irish, Scots, or Welsh. The game of darts and dart leagues is becoming quite a popular pastime in Kent County. The darts add to the atmosphere of the pub.

By seven o'clock I'd finished shooting most of my story; all that was left was to shoot some of the live entertainment that started just after nine. On Thursday, Friday and Saturday nights, the house band calling themselves "What" performs. Neil plays guitar and he's the lead member of this group of merry men. My sister Dana and a few people from her real estate office in Chatham came over to join Doug and me. Sam Kinsmen, a reporter/photographer for the *Wallaceburg News* joined us for dinner. He'd been around earlier in the afternoon to do a story on Doug, the home-town boy and me. It was a great night. A few months after we did the story, Sam Kinsmen passed away. Doug and I remember him fondly from that one happy experience we shared together at the Rovers Return in Wallaceburg.

In April of '94, Marilyn and Neil opened a second pub, located in the hamlet of Lighthouse Cove on the shores of Lake St. Clair. It's about thirty minutes west of Chatham. I popped in for a visit and a good feed of their fish and chips on one of my trips to that part of the province. Their new pub sits right next to a marina with a grand view of the boats during the summer months. On the first of January 1995, the Malcolm's sold their Wallaceburg establishment to Cindy Neil-Carr. The new owner has retained the same warm pub atmosphere, but has changed the name to Rovers End.

THE IRON DUKE

I was always fascinated by my Irish heritage and anyone with an accent from Ireland or Britain. A couple of my uncles married women from the U.K., so the British accent was around me from the time of my birth in 1942. My uncle Ivan Culbert married Aunt Elvira from Wales. She'd been an ambulance driver during the war when Uncle Ivan was overseas in the Canadian Army. My mother's brother, my uncle George Patrick, married Aunt Rosa from England. My first marriage was to Sarah Elizabeth Francis Veighey, born on the Isle of Wight in England. My daughters Sarah Jane and Dana Rose were the first born to the Veighey family on this side of the Atlantic. My cousin Campbell Culbert married an English woman who had come to Canada when she was just ten years old. Cam and Hazel have lived and worked as high school teachers in London, England for almost thirty years. They aren't returning to Canada after they retire because they've purchased a gorgeous two hundred-year-old cottage in the Cotswolds. It's in a small village called Fulbrook, near Burford in County Oxfordshire. There are no shops, but it does have two pubs. I love British pubs and their beer. As a result of all this, I have a passion for anything to do with Ireland and the British Isles. After taking my first trip to Northern Ireland and England in June of 1969, I've been across the ocean no fewer than thirteen times. One of my dreams is to take a holiday on board a narrowboat, travelling along Britain's canal system.

So, after telling you all that, you can see how excited I was when I happened to see an authentic-looking narrowboat putt-putting along the Rideau River near Kemptville, Ontario. I was just completing a story at the Ludlow Boat Works about Canada's oldest registered sailing yacht, *Canada*. As I peered out between a pair of drydocked boats, I saw it: a narrowboat gliding slowly through the calm waters, looking just like the ones I'd seen in Skipton, North Yorkshire. Phillip Ludlow told me that I'd find it downstream at the first set of locks. I put my gear away, said goodbye to Phillip, and went in search of this beautiful boat.

There it was, tied alongside the lock. It was magnificent, painted just like the ones in England. Called *The Iron Duke*, it was painted red, white, and green. It was exactly like the original canal barges that worked the English countryside, dating back to 1793. At one point during those early years, England had sixty-two different canal systems. It was the canals that drew England together. Raw materials and finished goods were conveyed between factories and ports. The canal boatmen and their families lived on board their boats; they had no home on land. If more than one child was born to a boat family, their tiny living quarters would get a little cramped.

David Brett is the owner and skipper of *The Iron Duke* and we chatted for a few minutes alongside his boat. He is from London, England, and took retirement from British Telecom. He'd fallen in love with narrowboats when he was thirty. His late wife Joyce, a Canadian, was working in Britain when they met. Joyce brought David back to Canada and introduced him to the Rideau Canal system. After they decided to move to Canada, David had an eleven-tonne, thirty-eight-foot Birmingham Canal Navigation Tug built in Birmingham. When it was completed, they had it shipped across the Atlantic to Montreal by freighter. From Montreal, it was transported along Highway 401 by flatbed transport to Kingston. Once, in the water, Joyce christened *The Iron Duke;* then the pair made their way up the Rideau to their home in the Merrickville area.

I set up a date to do the story with David. I did a three-day swing through Eastern Ontario, stopping in Brockville on the first day to do a story on "the house that pink pills built," Fulford House. Then it was on to Merrickville, where I'd booked two nights in a wonderful bed and breakfast on Mill Street. The two hundred-year-old village is really picturesque with its stone buildings and the Rideau Canal running right through the middle. David's home is on Kilmarnock Island, between Merrickville and Smiths Falls. To get onto the island itself, you just have to cross Kilmarnock Lock, the smallest lift in the Rideau Canal system, which raises and lowers the water level by just two feet. David's bungalow is filled with paintings and prints of the canal age in Britain. From the living room window I could see *The Iron Duke* tied to the dock.

I went on board with my television equipment. David started the three-cylinder air-cooled engine and cast off. "It's an expensive toy, but I really love it," said David. "People love it. They're forever coming up to me when I dock, just to chat. It's slow, not really suited for Canadian weather, with the winters and all, but I think it's wonderful and it adds a little bit of colour amongst the fibreglass boats that you see all around you today. I can tell people appreciate its beauty." Gliding along the waterway at three to four miles per hour, you get a chance to take in what nature has to offer. If I never fulfill my dream of a holiday on board a narrowboat in Britain, I will always cherish those hours spent with David Brett and his fantastic tug, *The Iron Duke*.

CELEBRATION OF LIGHTS

Situated on the St. Clair River, the port city of Sarnia is a key link in the St. Lawrence Seaway System. Each winter, from late November until early January, the city of 125,000 lights up for the Christmas season with its Celebration of Lights. Several things helped to inspire this concept. One was Canada's Chemical Valley. For years Canada's billion-dollar industry would light up to celebrate our Lord's birthday and the arrival of old St. Nick. People would come from miles around to view these fantastic light displays. The outline, ablaze with colour, could be seen from across the St. Clair River in neighbouring Port Huron, Michigan. Another source of inspiration came from Sarnia resident Harvey McMichael. Each year people would drive by or stop, get out and look at the way Harvey had decorated his home. Harvey McMichael passed away before the Celebration of Lights got into full swing. His spirit lives on in the hearts and minds of the people of Sarnia-Lambton.

Centennial Park, located on the downtown waterfront, is the focal point of the Celebration. It features a miniature village and tens of thousands of twinkling lights. I talked to Pat Laframboise, manager of the Sarnia-Lambton Visitor and Convention Bureau, which hosts the Celebration. "We're very interested in hydro consumption," she said, "and want to be power savers and energy savers. So we don't turn our park lights on until seven at night and we've asked the area home-owners to shut their lights off by eleven."

The Celebration is entirely funded by the many donations received from business, industry and organizations in the area. Over two hundred people of all ages volunteer their time every year to set up Centennial Park. The majority of the displays were designed and constructed by local clubs and organizations. The Visitor and Convention Bureau keeps the momentum of the festival going by having an annual lighting competition, when residents, business and industry vie for the winning entry. Competition is always intense, making it hard work for the judges. Visitors, especially those from American cities such as Cleveland and Detroit, are amazed at how whole neighbourhoods decorate their homes.

I did my story just before Christmas in 1991, on a beautiful, clear, but extremely cold night. In my television script I mentioned three homes. The first was that of the Pat Ryan family in Froomfield, between Sarnia and Corunna. The second home belonged to the Legeres family at the corner of Carr and Isabella in Sarnia itself. They were both well done. Then, as I drove through the suburbs, I came across that year's first-place winner in the residential category. At the bottom end of Seneca Court stood Bill and Julianne Vanderheuvel's house. It was truly amazing. The only time I really felt the cold was on this street, because I decided to wait for a bus tour to come along. Sarnia Transit hosts tours, and, the previous year, twenty-five hundred people took advantage of the warm way of seeing the lights. After the bus left, I did too. My left hand had become so darn cold that it brought tears to the eyes of the old boy. All I could think of was a hot bowl of soup and, by 9:30 p.m., I was sitting in the warmth of a Red Lobster restaurant enjoying a bowl of clam chowder.

The jaw of Ontario Northland's *Chi-Cheemaun* opens as she approaches the Tobermory Dock. 1994 marked twenty years of service for this magnificent ship.

CHI-CHEEMAUN'S 20th BIRTHDAY

Quite often, as youngsters, my sister Dana and I would travel with our parents for a summer holiday to Manitoulin Island. We'd travel from our home in Lucan to Tobermory where we'd board the *Norgoma* or the *Norisle*. This was an exciting event as the passenger cars drove up the ramp and into the coal-fired ship. I remember one crossing being particularly rough and I became quite queasy. My father suggested that we all go have a meal. That certainly did the trick, because I was fine for the remainder of the voyage. I have a vivid memory of that dining room, the tables covered with linen cloths, fine china and quality silverware. The waiters were handsomely dressed. Those were the good old days. When we took this route, we were going to visit my Aunt Margaret and her family. My mother's younger sister was married to Dave Glover, a New Brunswicker who had come west to work. In the town of Little Current my uncle and aunt bought the General Motors garage called Acme Motors. The garage is still in the family today; it's now run by my cousin Larry.

In August of '94, I was crossing over to the Island again, not on vacation this time; I was going to do a number of stories in the region. The two old ships had been replaced by Ontario Northland's premier ferry, the *Chi-Cheemaun*, built in 1974 in the Collingwood Shipyard. The 365-foot vessel was celebrating twenty years of transporting passengers and motor vehicles from the Tobermory dock to South Baymouth on Manitoulin Island. I just couldn't pass up the opportunity to do a story on her. I arrived in Tobermory at 10:30 a.m. She was due in from Manitoulin just before eleven. I positioned myself on the far side of the harbour, setting up my tripod and camera. Scuba divers were searching the clear water in front of me for lost wrecks. Right on schedule, the magnificent ship rounded the point. With my telephoto lens, I shot scenes of her coming in and manoeuvering into the dock. Once secured, the hydraulic bow-visor, known to children as "Jaws," opened to enable the cars in her belly to come out and a new load of vehicles to go in. If you've never seen this sight, it's well worth a trip, even if you don't take the voyage.

A few weeks before I left, I talked to Captain Leath Davis by phone. He's the Director of Marine Services, headquartered in Owen Sound. Captain Davis had arranged for me to meet Tobermory Terminal Superintendant Allan Shaw who would be my interview subject for the story. Allan joined Ontario Northland's Marine Services in 1969.

The young farmboy who had grown up on the Bruce has fond memories of the day the *Chi-Cheemaun* first came into service. "I was one of the wheelsmen aboard the ship when it first came in. That was a highlight in itself, but just the awe of the new ship compared to the two old ones. It was just such a big gorgeous ship when it first came into port at Tobermory."

After we'd finished the interview, Allan told me that Captain Davis was driving up from Owen Sound and would probably be taking the voyage to South Baymouth and back. Every once in a while he does that just to observe and ensure that everything is running smoothly. Captain Davis arrived, and he and Allan took me to lunch.

By mid-afternoon the *Chi-Cheemaun* had returned. When the signal was given, the long lines of waiting cars, trucks, and motorcycles drove into the parking quarters aboard the huge vessel. Her capacity is 140 standard North American automobiles and just under 650 passengers. I met up with Captain Davis and the ship's steward, Jim Stitt. Jim took me down below where the passengers can't go, down to the spotlessly clean engine room. Two 3500-horsepower Ruston diesels drove us across the open waters. Cruising speed is sixteen and a quarter knots or twenty miles per hour. The trip from Tobermory to South Baymouth takes just under two hours.

The *Chi-Cheemaun* is the flagship of Ontario Northland's ferry fleet. She's also the largest passenger vehicle vessel on the Great Lakes. Up top, on the bridge, Captain Charlie Shaw was the man in charge. He's Allan's older brother and joined the company in 1965. Ontario Northland employs 112 people between the two ports and the crew of 32 change twice daily.

Crossing Georgian Bay on the *Chi-Cheemaun* is a wonderful experience, no matter what your age. It's also a great shortcut to the north during the summer holidays. As the ship enters her third decade, the *Chi-Cheemaun* will run every day from early May until mid-October.

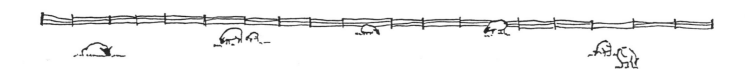

Terrence Patrick Culbert in the land of his ancestors

Photograph: Wayne Brennan

VILLAGE NAME

Do you ever wonder where many of the place names in our province come from? Obvious names like London and Stratford are the names of cities in England. Even the rivers that flow through them, the Thames in London and the Avon in Stratford, were given the old-country names. In northern Ontario, the town of Kapuskasing took its name from an Indian word meaning "the divided waters" or "bend in the river." The one I've often wondered about was the village of Lucan, where I grew up. I knew it had been settled by the Irish in the 1800s, but had it been named after a person, perhaps Lord Lucan, or was it a place name in Ireland? Well, years ago, I found it on a map. It wasn't far from Dublin in southern Ireland.

In November of 1989, I travelled to the olde sod with my brother-in-law Wayne Brennan. On this pleasurable trip, Wayne's first to Ireland, we visited some of his relatives. Just before we left, I was talking to his Aunt Gen and she filled me in on the family. I learned that Wayne had a cousin over there. I told Wayne the good news. We didn't tell the cousin we were coming and just showed up at the farm. At first, James and Nora Kelly thought we travelling salesmen. After we explained that we were Aunt Gen Brennan's nephews, they wouldn't hear of us travelling anymore that day. "It'll soon be dark and the roads to Galway are full of curves," said James. "You'd best stay on till mornin'." So, we stayed with James and his family in Ballymurry, County Roscommon. We had such a wonderful time that we didn't leave the farm until late the following morning.

On this trip we passed through and stopped in Lucan, twice. I believe that my Irish ancestors from County Tip-perary must have travelled east to Dublin City and, if they did, they'd surely have taken the route along the River Liffey. This river rises in the Wicklow Mountains, then meanders past the pretty village of Lucan before flowing through Dublin to the Irish Sea. The village of Lucan is situated eight miles to the west of Dublin. As Wayne and I wandered about taking a few still photographs, I told him that someday I'd return with my television camera and do a story on the two villages with the same name.

In May of '93, Global's Bob McAdorey and I travelled to Ireland and I did just that. Accompanied by our host and escort John Kennedy of the Irish Tourist Board, we drove to Lucan early one Sunday morning. Growing up in Dublin, John used to hike to this village with his brother for ice cream. The population has grown a lot since John was a boy. As a bedroom community to the Republic's largest city, Lucan has gone from a population of two thousand to sixteen thousand in the past decade.

While capturing this pretty Irish village on videotape, I met Martin Monoghan. The seventy-two-year-old retired roads worker had worked for the village council all his life. His parents were gardeners at a huge estate in the centre of the village, now the official residence of the Italian Ambassador. "Oh well, ya hadn't the population a quarter the size it is now," says Martin. "You've sixteen thousand population now. At one time I knew everyone at that end of the town to that end of town, now I don't know them at all."

It's hard to believe that in the past two hundred and fifty years more than six million Irish have left their homeland. That's a million more than live in all of Ireland today. The

My brother-in law Wayne Brennan in Lucan, County Dublin, Ireland. Lucan, Ontario was named after this Irish village.

major emigration began in 1815 after the Napoleonic Wars. Even before the Great Potato Famines of the mid-1840s, thousands had already left their country for the new world. Many came to Canada, hundreds settling in south-western Ontario's Biddulph Township. Here they knew they'd be able to purchase land. These early settlers also knew there'd be a lot of hard work ahead, clearing the land of trees so that they'd be able to till the soil and grow their crops. They came to the new world for the benefit of their families, believing that life would be much better in this country. My own family was part of this group, emigrating just before the famine struck. They left Ballymackey, a small farming community to the east of Nenaugh, Tipperary. John Culbert had been married to Mary Ward for five years

before they left for Canada. They came to Biddulph Township in 1840. John and Mary were buried in St. James Cemetery halfway between Lucan and Clandeboye. Their gravestone still stands, but the lettering has worn away with time.

Like so many of the early pioneers, the settlers named their new villages after places they'd left behind. Lucan, Ontario was one of those places. The population was nine hundred when I left home in 1961. Over the next three decades Lucan grew, not near as much as the Irish Lucan, but it did double in size. It's a bedroom community for those that work in nearby London, though it still remains true to its beginnings as a farming community. My uncle Mert Culbert, one of my father's five brothers, was born on the farm that our family bought from the Canada Company in Toronto when they first arrived. He has the original sales receipt from that transaction. I included Uncle Mert in the story and, as he showed the historic document, he said: "It's dated October tenth, 1840 and this was when my great grandfather came from Tipperary, Ireland and purchased the land in Biddulph Township. For the hundred acres of land just to the northwest of Lucan, John Culbert paid sixty-two pounds, ten shillings." Uncle Mert and my darling aunt Muriel (Hardy) Culbert sold the farm a number of years ago and moved into the village. That brought to an end four generations of Culberts on the farm.

My story also needed a local historian and Uncle Mert suggested a friend of his named Hamilton Hodgins. I hadn't seen Hamilton since I was a teenager. After retiring from his farm, he and his wife and son moved into Lucan. Hamilton has spent years writing the history of his own family and of the Lucan area as well. Looking me straight in the eye, Hamilton said, "Of all the Culberts, including your grandfather's six sons, you look the most like him. You're a dead-ringer for old Myron." To me, this was a real compliment.

The amateur historian is the great-great-grandson of the first white settler in Biddulph Township. "Big Jim" Hodgins arrived in 1832 from Tipperary with his wife Mary and their eight children. As the local agent for the Canada Company, "Big Jim" became known as the founder of Biddulph, and was the driving force in settling the area.

Uncle Mert and Aunt Muriel Culbert, along with my sister Dana Garrett in St. James cemetery near Lucan, Ontario. This tombstone belongs to my great-great-grandparents, John and Mary (Ward) Culbert. They'd come to Canada in 1840 from Tipperary, Ireland.

The author at twelve years of age (1954). Lucan Public School photograph.

"I'm sure that these early settlers were very proud indeed," said Hamilton. "When they got to the stage where they saw their children having horses of their own to work with and owning a whole farm; seeing them progress from the little log shanties that they started with to good substantial buildings and properous farms." To find my village namesake in Lucan, County Dublin and to walk the Irish soil that my ancestors left behind one hundred and fifty years ago was an incredible experience for me, one that I'll never forget.

I'm also very proud to have been raised in Lucan, Ontario, to have grown up there during the '40s and '50s. There was a freedom that I'm sure children of the city never experienced. We made our own fun. Before the arena was constructed, we'd play hockey on Shipley's pond or next to the storage shed at Scott's Grain Elevator. We were only two teams, the Toronto Maple Leafs and the Montreal Canadiens. In the summer, we'd skinny-dip at Rock Bottom, a deep pool in the Little Ausable River. We even had a motion picture projectionist bring movies to the village and show them to us in the opera house above Stanley's Drug Store. The original Lassie movies were real weepers. We learned to drive with our fathers on the gravel back roads. And we had romantic crushes on girls who didn't even know we existed, especially if we were chubby with curly hair. What the heck, I had crushes on them all. There was Beth, Laverne, Anne and her sister Rose; there was Anne-Marie, Heather, Judy, Bonnie, Marnie, Julia, Carol and her sister Joan. I wouldn't trade growing up in my Irish-Canadian village for anything.

Two young ladies in Lucan that made a young man's heart flutter were Heather Acheson and Judy Haskett. I photographed the two Medway High School cheerleaders in 1960 for the *Exeter Times-Advocate*.

Culbert.

BELL TOWER WRITINGS

In 1992 a discovery was made and printed in the *London Free Press*. It seems that countless generations of bellringers and repairmen left a record of great and not-so-great moments in history on the interior walls of St. Paul's Cathedral bell tower in London, Ontario. St. Paul's is the mother church of the Diocese of Huron. On her grounds a few tombstones remain from the British Army garrison that was there in the early 1800s. The nave and church tower were constructed in 1845 in an English Gothic Revival style. The stone used for the gargoyles was brought over from the same stone quarry that Sir Christopher Wren used while building St. Paul's Cathedral in London, England.

This was definitely a story for me. I was met at the cathedral by John Allen and his wife Maisie. The retired couple are quite involved with the church as Maisie's a tour guide and her husband John, a former tool-and die maker, is the present bellringer. It took a few minutes to bring all my camera gear up to the loft because the wooden steps were long and very narrow. We were eventually joined by the dean of St. Paul's, the Very Reverend Bruce Howe. When I looked around, it was like looking at the pages of a history book. Events had been recorded for over a century. On the wooden door a notation read: "Canadian Contingent left here October 25th, 1899, for South Africa." On the walls I found and videotaped the following: "President McKinley shot in Buffalo." "September 30th, 1899 . . . snow on ground fell to the depth of four inches on the level." Reverend Howe read this from an opposite wall: "Now, the funeral of King George the 5th and it also mentions the invasion of Italy. And then Italy surrenders. Here's a mention of the Red Army offensive opening in Korea in 1951. Here's another, Russia at war."

Maisie Allen found one by a former bellringer: "Mr. Kingsmill recorded how he rang the bells every New Year's all the way through, but when he got to here, when the war came, no chimes . . . no chimes. But then suddenly in '43, he did ring them on New Year's and then he started ringing them again all the way down here to '50 . . . what's that, '51, '53 . . . he rang them every New Year. Over the years many marriages were recorded by the bellringers: "Miss Smith married September 26th 1891 to Mr. Rowley of Berlin, Ontario."

Unfortunately, for safety reasons, the general public will never get to see these writings, except in newspaper features from the *London Free Press*, or on television stories like mine. One of the reasons I love my job so much is because I can go to places that sometimes are off limits to the public.

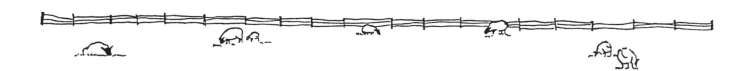

London Wines 15,000 square foot corporate centre on historic
"Winery Hill."

Photograph courtesy of London Winery Limited

LONDON WINES

A large colour spread in the *London Free Press* caught my attention. It was an article about London Wines and a photograph of a new building. It was their new 15,000 square foot, tudor-style corporate centre and touring facility. On the same page was a congratulatory note from Tonda Construction, the general contractor that built the building. My oldest friend, Tom Weller, is Tonda Construction. Tom and I became close buddies from the day we met at the age of ten. After we'd both completed high school, we took our first apartment together in London. Tom was an apprentice carpenter with Ellis-Don Construction, and I worked on *Romper Room* in the morning and in the newsroom during the afternoon at CFPL Television. Feeling extremely proud of my old chum, I just had to do a story on the winery, so that I could show off Tom's handiwork.

Nicknamed Winery Hill, the section of Wharncliffe Road South in London has been home to the London Winery, vintners, and wine merchants, since 1925. The history of the winery can be traced back to the year 1871. Canada's first winery, the Hamilton Dunlop Winery was established in Brantford, by Major J. S. Hamilton, the dean of Canada's wine makers. It was purchased by the London Winery in 1945.

As I brought my equipment into the reception room of the new building, I was impressed with the coziness of the area. In the centre was a fireplace surrounded by comfortable couches and Queen Anne chairs. A large mirror sat atop the fireplace mantle, stained-glass panels adorning its sides. The glass was lit from behind, bringing out the very colourful stained-glass grape design. This is the area were the in-depth winery tours and educational seminars begin.

London Winery was established by the Knowles brothers, Arthur Neville and Joseph Chamberlain. Evelyn, wife of Arthur Neville Knowles, was appointed president in 1942 upon the passing of both the company founders. Today, Evelyn's son Pete and his children operate the winery. I met public relations co-ordinator Deborah Walsh and asked her if it would be possible to do an interview with one or two family members. It was an unfortunate time because everyone but the president was away on business and she didn't think he'd appear on camera because he was shy. Not one to give up, I asked her if it would be possible to see him face to face, so that I could explain what I was doing? She agreed and, without my camera, we paid a visit to the president's office. I met the tall, handsome man. It turned out that he had a good sense of humour and I explained to Pete that I only needed a couple of scenes of him, no interview. He agreed. Outside his office, in the hallway of the original building, I photographed President Pete and Deborah checking out an old bottle from their archives.

The winery operates public tours seven days a week and will accommodate as few as two or as many as a bus load of wine enthusiasts. On my personal tour, Deborah showed me the oldest wine barrel in their cellar. Filled with Chardonnay, the oak cask had originally been used aboard a ship as far back as 1871. In another area of the wine cellar I met Jim Patience. The wine maker is a native of Edinburgh, Scotland, where he began his career in a brewery. He came to Canada in his early twenties and has been with London Wines for over three decades. Standing in front of some wooden casks he did an interview for me. "In this American oak," said Jim, "we're aging the sherry. It will be aged here for about eight years. London Wines is one of the last

Photograph: Donna Culbert

My friend for over forty years, general contractor Tom Weller
and me at his daughter Tracy's wedding in 1990.

remaining wineries in Canada producing fine sherries and
ports."

In the bottling section of the plant, something relatively
new was happening. Their Westminster Sherry is now
bottled in clear plastic containers. The new lightweight
bottle is extremely popular with seniors, and it's recyclable.
Deborah took me to the quality control laboratories where
it was evident that wine making is both an art and a science.
"For many years Canadian wine has gotten a bad rap for
quality, taste and even some of our packaging," said Deborah. "In recent years, since we started growing the French
hybrids, our wines have won many international awards.
Probably Canada's most recent recognition has been ice
wine, especially here in Ontario."

Grapes for normal table wines are harvested in September, but grapes for ice wine are picked in sub-zero temperatures, usually in January. At London Wines' own

vineyard near Cedar Springs on the north shore of Lake
Erie, the grapes must freeze on the vine at least three times
before they're picked. With each freezing, the sugar inside
the grape concentrates, giving this wine its distinctive
flavour. The wine is almost as thick as a liqueur. The sugar
content is nineteen and a half percent compared to one to
four, for a dinner wine.

I ended my story in front of the camera, sitting next to
the fireplace. I held a glass of Ancient Mead, a wine that
brought back memories of living in London in my twenties.
Then I talked to the camera about how Mead is made with
honey, and that the London Winery is the only producer
of Ancient Mead in North America. Its origins date back
to 300 B.C., when it was customary for young German
newlyweds to celebrate their love by drinking it for thirty
days following the wedding ceremony; hence the word
"Honeymoon."

Photograph courtesy of London Winery Limited

London Wines is one of the last remaining winery's in Canada producing fine sherries and ports.

This photograph of Andy Cole was taken by his sister Rosie in 1919 at their parents' farm near Norwich, Ontario. Twenty-eight-year-old Andy is holding Polly, the white horse and Kit, the Dapple.

103rd BIRTHDAY

Dawn Collins, an editorial assistant in our newsroom, was in the middle of a long-distance phone call as I passed by her desk. I had just packed up and was heading home for dinner when she called out to me. She said that a woman on the other end of the line wanted to know if Global was interested in doing a story on her grandfather who was going to be 103 in the next couple of days.

Over the phone I learned that Janice Carpenter had come home to visit her mother Marie in Simcoe. She'd also come home to celebrate her grandfather Andy Cole's 103rd birthday. As we spoke, I took a few notes. Janice told me that her Grandad was as sharp as a razor and lived in Simcoe

with his son Tom and his daughter-in-law Teresa. I told Janice that I wouldn't be able to do the story on the actual birthday, but I'd set it up for a few days later. After a couple of telephone calls to Teresa, I'd set up a time and a date.

I travel the province almost always by myself but, on this day, my mother-in-law Mary Brennan accompanied me. I was able to drop her off for a visit with her niece Mary Jean Kokus and family. They also live in this Haldiman-Norfolk town. The traffic that summer morning was light. After dropping off Mother Mary, I drove over to the Cole residence almost an hour early. Son Tom answered the door-bell and it was quite obvious that he'd just stepped out of the shower. Not far behind his father was two-year-old Sean and his older sister Caitlin. People must hate me for being early, but it's just one of my little quirks; I don't like to keep people waiting. Tom graciously took me through the house to meet his father. There at the kichen sink, sitting on a tall stool, was a little man looking very much like an Irish leprechaun. He was washing up the breakfast dishes.

Andy was born the 6th of July, 1891, the middle child of thirteen children born to Mary Broadley and Edward Cole on a farm in Round Plains near Waterford, Ontario. He nearly died of typhoid fever when he was thirty. His doctor told him that, if he lived through it, he probably be healthier than he ever was. The doctor was right. Andy stayed on to farm with his parents, raising pure-bred Holstein dairy cattle. One of his true loves was breaking and showing horses. He claims that farming was hard work before modern machinery came along. Andy bought his first tractor just after the Second World War. His parents were married seventy-one years and both lived into their nineties. After his parents died, he kept the dairy farm near Norwich going until he was in his early sixties, then he retired. He got bored staying at home and ended up working for a tobacco farmer until he was eighty-eight.

Andy married when he was sixty-three, in 1955. He married Lillian, a forty-year-old widow with a daughter called Marie. Marie is the mother of Janice Carpenter, the lady who called Global. Andy and Lillian bought a house on Washington Street in Waterford, where he spent the next thirty-four years. A year after they married, Lillian gave birth to son Tom. Just for the record, Andy's sister Nina is 104 and lives on her own in Brantford, and his sister Gladys is 91 and lives in Delhi. Andy is a great fan of the Toronto Maple Leafs and the Toronto Blue Jays. On his hundredth birthday, he attended a game at the Skydome. At one point during the game, a happy birthday wish to him appeared on the Jumbotron and everyone in the stadium sang "Happy Birthday.'"

Andy remembers the first automobile he ever saw. It was chain driven and so noisy that it scared the horses. He also remembers that, in the days of large families and close-knit communities, the Sunday socials at the church were the main social event. What's his secret for longevity? He admits that genes probably have something to do with it. A life of hard work on the farm didn't hurt either. Then he said to me: "Well, I don't know. I guess the good Lord. Yup, it's through the good Lord." Andy never smoked and never drank. Was he ever tempted, I asked? "Oh, I've been tempted as far as that goes, but I generally refused it." He went on to say that, on a hot day, the tobacco farmer who he worked for was known to bring him back a bottle of nice cold beer. Hey, I don't see anything wrong with that. And, by the way, he was well over sixty at the time.

When you reach the age of 103, it's a big event down in Haldiman-Norfolk County. Lifestyle editor Cheryl Bauslaugh of the *Simcoe Reformer* gave Andy's story a half page with photographs. What a wonderful experience it was for me to meet Andy Cole. I only wish I could have made my story with him a little longer. I'm darn sure he'd have an awful lot more to say.

Pining 4U's Ethel and Arthur Levman, with woodworking apprentice Mark Allen. I could have sworn there were two dogs here when I took this photo.

PRIDE IN SERVICE

Stephanie Black had just returned from visiting her father at his condominium in Thornbury. Stephanie, a co-host for three years on Global's *Kids Beat* and now our fashion reporter, was excited about a store that she and her father had been in, called Pining 4U. Stephanie told me how wonderful and thoughtful the owners were. Unlike a lot of stores today, the couple that owns this shop actually treat their customers like royalty. She told me that Ethel and Arthur Levman take pride in the service that they provide.

I visited the Georgian Bay village, which has a population of fifteen hundred. In an old house along Highway 26 on the eastern outskirts of Thornbury, the Levmans had opened their store with the primary intention of making and selling handcrafted pine furniture. When they discovered that their customers needed furnishings as well, they expanded, filling three rooms with wonderful accessories. Ethel went back to school in the early eighties and received her interior design degree and now gives free design services to their customers. The Levmans are truly from the old school when it comes to caring for their customers' needs. "I'm always enquiring of customers," Ethel said, "where are you from? What do you do? Or, what are you doing in this area? I enjoy meeting people and we do have a lot of customers who keep coming back, so our service must mean something. They seem to care about Arthur and me

and they address us as Arthur and Ethel. They just don't come into a cold store."

Then Arthur said, "Mind you, there's one fact though, ninety percent of our business is repeat and referral, at least ninety percent. In fact they come in knowing us rather than the product." Another attraction at this delightful shop are their two adorable hounds. In the crowded aisles, you literally have to step over Buddy and Napoleon. As I moved my lights and tripod from room to room, they seemed totally unaware that I was even there.

In the kitchen to the rear of the store I caught up with Ethel as she was gift wrapping a present for Dr. Sean Lawes. The Collingwood veterinarian and his young son Stephen were buying a present for Stephen's mother. Ethel personally wraps each gift for the customer free of charge. "If the gift is five dollars or five hundred dollars," said Ethel, "it goes out of here looking like the Taj Mahal."

From a background in the Toronto building trade, Arthur learned cabinetmaking by watching old country tradesmen. He's now passing on his knowledge to a local lad named Mark Allen. Arthur and Ethel are totally satisfied with their lifestyle in the Thornbury area, and pleasing their customers is all-important to them. And just as Stephanie Black had told me, Arthur and Ethel were a delight.

BLUE DIAMOND ANNIVERSARY

One can't imagine a village or town in Europe, Britain or Ireland that is only seventy-five years old. But here in Canada, especially the north, this is not unusual. One such place celebrated its seventy-fifth anniversary in July of 1994, the northern Ontario mining town of Kirkland Lake. I made the seven-and-a-half-hour trek in June to do a preview story on the anniversary. Because of the distance, and to make the trip economically worthwhile, I did two other stories as well. The second was on the Museum of Northern History and the third on raku potter Bonnie Borden.

I arrived in town late Monday afternoon, still early enough to touch base with the folks at the museum. While there, it was pointed out that a local author had written a book about the town to coincide with the anniversary. I made a mental note of this and planned to get a shot of the book and perhaps the author working on his computer. From the museum, I made my way downtown to the *Northern Daily News*. I wanted to say hello to Bernd Franke. Bernd is a thirty-eight-year-old career journalist who runs the newsroom for this Thompson paper. I told Bernd that for each story I must have a "talking-head." This is normally the person I'm doing the story about, but I was having trouble locating someone to interview for the anniversary story. Perhaps what I needed was an old prospector or maybe the mayor.

Bernd suggested an old retired newspaper man who had been around these parts forever. As I was mulling the possibilities over, I asked him if he knew how to get hold of the author of the book that I'd just seen for the first time at the museum. "Michael Barnes," Bernd said, "why, he lives just outside town. Good night to give him a call, Terry,

because it's his wife's night out." How in the world did this guy know that Michael would be home alone because his wife was going out? After I'd checked into the Bon Air Motor Inn, I gave Michael a call. "Come on out," he said, "It's my wife's night out with the ladies. They're quilting."

At his lakeside home, as we sat and chatted, I learned that Michael is northern Ontario's only full-time commercial writer, and to date has had three-dozen books published. *Kirkland Lake: On the Mile of Gold* was his latest. As we talked I knew that this was the person I wanted as my "talking-head." The fifty-nine-year-old retired public school principal was a walking, talking and breathing encyclopedia of all things northern. The author/historian was witty and turned out to be totally relaxed in front of my camera.

Michael was not from Kirkland Lake; he was an outsider. Born in Surrey, England, he'd emigrated to Canada in 1956 and has lived in the north ever since. Before darkness set in, we drove to town and Michael gave me a guided tour of the locations that he thought might be interesting. We ended our evening conversing over a couple of beers and a big bowl of popcorn at the Bellevue Tavern. The owners refer to their place as Kirkland Lake's finest old English-style pub. The establishment is owned by two delightful ladies, Monica Rankin and Lorraine Robazza. They were separate schoolteachers together. Monica still teaches, but Lorraine decided to take early retirement.

On Tuesday, I did the story of Sir Harry Oakes and his old home that is now the Museum of Northern History. Wednesday morning, Michael and I met and had a hearty breakfast at his favourite restaurant on Government Road. It's interesting how Kirkland Lake got its name. It seems that in the early part of this century a land surveyor named

Malcolm MacPherson, a former manager of Macassa Mine and his wife Mary, took shelter from the rain as they watched the memorial parade and service Thursday, July 12.

L. P. Rorke discovered a small lake and decided to name it after Winnie Kirkland, a secretary in his office back in Toronto. Winnie never did come north to see the lake that was named after her.

Michael and I made our way around town taking shots of workers and machines as they rebuilt sidewalks and streets in preparation for the upcoming festivities. Vacant lots that once housed stores destroyed by fire were now little parkettes with grass and trees. Over at the town hall, I took a few scenes of Michael talking to the very colourful and long-serving Mayor Joe Mavrinac. I asked Michael why he'd titled his book *On the Mile of Gold*. "Terry, I use the term 'mile of gold' because that's what this was," he said. "One mile, and on it, spaced out, seven great gold mines producing millions of dollars worth of gold every year."

From the guided tour that Michael had given me two nights before, I chose three sites that would make interesting components in my story. At each of the locations, I put the tiny neck microphone on Michael, who stood looking at the lens of the camera as he delivered his lines. He was really good and, without notes, he delivered these lines: "To the uninitiated, this looks like the Sahara Desert. But it isn't sand; this is slimes or mine tailings. This is all that's left of forty-two-million ounces of gold that was produced in the heyday of Kirkland Lake. And the slimes that I'm holding, well, two percent of them are solid twenty-four-carat gold."

Then we drove to the village of Swastika where I placed him in front of the old Swastika Hotel. Michael continued: "This is Swastika, the only one in the world. It's now part of Kirkland Lake, but seventy years ago prospectors first, and then miners, jumped off the train here and went east to the gold fields. Some of them, well, they found fame and fortune, others just a lifetime of work—underground." Our final destination was atop a hill with a working mine in the background. Michael chose Lac Minerals' Macassa Mine. Once again he delivered his lines to the camera: "This is Macassa Mine, the last of the seven great gold mines in Kirkland Lake. Below the ground here you have the equivalant of four CN Towers standing end to end. Imagine, eight thousand feet, the deepest single-lift shaft in North America."

Well, it was time to take a coffee break at Tim Horton's. As we sat there, I noticed a woman slipping a note under my windshield wiper. It had to be an advertisement, maybe a discount car wash, because the wagon was pretty dirty. As the woman turned to leave, I shouted out, "That's Lynn McLellan." Jumping up from the table, I caught up with her and her aunt Elisa Cole just before they drove away. Lynn is the wife of my friend and colleague from Global, Doug McLellan. She was passing through enroute to her uncle and aunt's cottage near Rouyn-Noranda, Quebec. She'd noticed the Global station wagon at the doughnut shop but couldn't find me inside.

After our break, we finished off the story with a sequence of the *Northern Daily News*. The area's only daily which has been publishing for seventy-three years. Michael and I made arrangements to go out on assignment with photographer/reporter Rick Owen. We drove to the new Miners Memorial Monument which was being erected on the western edge of town. The monument is dedicated to all the miners have worked in one of the greatest gold mining camps in all of the world. I took shots of Rick taking pictures of the men working for my story and he did an article on what I was doing in the north. It worked out well for both of us. There definitely is a quality of life in the north that one does not find in the city. There was something magical about being there.

Michael Barnes was recently awarded the Order of Canada for his contribution to the record of northern Ontario history. His next book, *Great Northern Characters,* was published by General Store Publishing House in 1994.

Photograph courtesy of Rick Owen/Northern Daily News

Bill Chase, of Logon Lake, B.C., who moved away from Swastika in 1943, admires the tribute to miners monument while standing next to a statue of local miner, Herb Boudreau.

Photograph courtesy of Barbara and Romoe Restorick

Adult female bison at the Buffalo Head Ranch near Ridgetown

BUFFALO DAYS

For over half a century I've travelled along Highway 2, then later Highway 401, to reach Chatham and Windsor, first as a boy with my family and then later on as a driver myself. In all that time, not once did I veer to the south a few miles to discover Ridgetown. With its population of 3300, Ridgetown claims to be the "friendliest town in Ontario." Well, I finally had the opportunity of visiting Ridgetown after receiving a letter from Mary Hemming, inviting me down to do a story on an event the town holds each July called "Buffalo Days." Mary, who's on the organizing committee for the four-day festival, thought perhaps a little exposure on Global Television would help with their attendance.

The farming community is home to Pioneer Seeds and the Ridgetown College of Agricultural Technology. The Kent County town was incorporated in 1875, although many of its gorgeous homes were built before that. One of those houses has become the town's museum. Ridge House was built in the 1870s as a middle-class home. And it was there that I met Elsie Reynolds, the museum curator and events co-ordinator for the town. "Ridgetown always wanted to have a festival of its own," she said. "We tried to come up with a theme and a name that was unique, different and appealing. Then it dawned on us—we have this wonderful buffalo ranch right on the edge of town. It seemed perfect. With the permission and co-operation of the owners, Romoe and Barbara Restorick, Buffalo Days was born."

Out at the ranch I met the Restoricks. They were just loading a group of high school students onto a tractor-drawn wagon, so I joined them. The young ladies would be given a short course in the art of tour guiding by Barbara for the up-coming festival. As the gate closed behind us, we bumped and thumped through 195 acres of pastureland.

The Buffalo Head Ranch started out as a hobby farm, but by the mid-80s it turned into a full-time business venture. Barbara and her husband Romoe raise more than just buffalo on their farm. They have Russian wild boar, elk, European red deer, English fallow, and whitetail deer. They have a camel named Simon, miniature donkeys, wild turkeys, peacocks, llamas, and Betty, a five-year-old white-tailed deer. At one point I jumped down from the wagon to get a better shot of this tiny critter. She boldly walked right up and stuck her nose into my camera lens. As I walked backwards, recording this moment on tape, she stayed right with me, allowing me to rub her neck with my left hand.

As Romoe drove to the back of their ranch, we caught sight of what the festival is all about. Grazing near a stand of trees was the herd of buffalo, numbering 130 in all. They're made up of Plains, Wood, and European bison. A full-grown bison can live twenty-five to thirty years, and can weigh as much as three thousand pounds. That's a ton and a half. Using a battery-operated megaphone, Barbara told the would-be-guides: "These are civilized animals, they're not domesticated animals. We leave them alone and they do just fine until you're ready to test them or something. They don't like to be handled."

As we left the contented herd, Romoe brought us to the centre of the farm where a small group of elk were grazing. Barbara once again spoke through her megaphone: "Now, of all the animals, the elks are smarter than the buffalo. They're also more dangerous."

This wagon ride had been quite an experience, even for an old guy like me. Ridgetown's "Buffalo Days" take place in mid-July each year, but the Buffalo Head Ranch takes tours from May through October.

Watercolour painting of the Kenney Hotel in Jones Falls done by F. H. Taylor in 1896. Original hangs in the lobby of Hotel Kenney, Jones Falls.

JONES FALLS AND THE KENNEY HOTEL

Global news producer Ian Blair asked me if I'd ever been to Jones Falls. When I said no and didn't even know where it was, he proceeded to fill me in on the history of this wonderful area of Ontario. He told me about the falls themselves and the old family-run hotel that sat nearby. Ian and his family have dined there regularly for years.

On an August day in 1992, I drove to the tiny community of Jones Falls, just to the north of Kingston. When I came upon the Kenney Hotel, it was like stepping back fifty years. With my reservation made, I arranged to do a story on the falls and the hotel over the next two days. After checking in, I stepped out onto the long, enclosed sunporch and from that vantage point I could see the Rideau Canal in front of me. The Canadian Parks Service continues to open and close the locks with handwinches. It's a tradition that the lockkeepers have maintained since 1832 when the canal opened.

The Rideau Canal was conceived in the wake of the War of 1812. It was constructed as a safe military route for the British in the event of an American attack along the St. Lawrence River though, in the end, it was never used for its intended purpose. In 1826, England sent Lieutenant Colonel John By, of the Royal Engineers, to supervise canal construction. Thousands of Irish immigrants and French-Canadian labourers pushed the canal route through the rough bush, swamps, and rocky wilderness of eastern Ontario. We tend to take these magnificent structures on the Rideau Canal for granted, but hundreds of men perished while it was being built, some from malaria and others from construction accidents.

Sitting high above the locks at Jones Falls is Sweeney House. It's one of the last defensible lock-master's homes on the entire canal system. Gunslits were constructed in the thick rubble walls to fend off attacks. One hundred and twenty blacksmith shops once stood along the waterway, stretching from Kingston to Ottawa. Today, only one remains and it's here at Jones Falls. It's difficult to imagine the hardships that four thousand men must have endured over the six years, as they contructed the two-hundred-kilometre route.

Colonel By hired a Scottish masonry contractor named John Redpath to build a 350-foot-long dam and four locks at Jones Falls. The great stone arch dam had the distinction of being the highest in North America at that time. With a height of sixty-two feet, it was also the first arch dam on this continent, in Britain or in France as well. The sandstone blocks used in this enormous project were drawn to the site by teams of oxen from a quarry six miles away. Today, Gananoque Light and Power use the excess water from the canal to produce hydro electricity. This area of Ontario is a definite must to visit, and within walking distance of the canal is the Kenney Hotel.

From the beginning the Kenney Hotel has been owned and operated by the same family. In 1877, Thomas Bartlett Kenney, a native of County Wexford, Ireland, built the clapboard structure. Thomas and his wife Eleanor Donohue originally operated it as a hotel, general store, and post office. Then, in 1906, they built an annex across the road and the store and post office were relocated there.

For over one hundred years it's been a popular destination for fishermen. The hotel supplied both guides and boats if needed.

A 1920's brochure for the hotel advertised it as "a paradise for anglers, with no black-flies and no hay fever."

Today, Joe Kenney is the fourth generation to operate the business. He's the founder's great-grandson. "The thing I hear the guests from the year before say as they step through the front door is, 'everything is the same as when we left. We feel like we're back home. It's like coming back to grandpa's.' They feel it's a step back to the '40s and '50s."

Many notables have stayed here, including William Howard Taft, the twenty-seventh President of the United States of America. He would come up to Canada and stay at the Kenney Hotel on many occasions with his fishing buddies. "One of the stories about President Taft that always gave us a chuckle was the fact that he was large. He was quite tall and a very heavy man," said Joe. "Our beds weren't large enough for him, so his own bed was brought along. It was quite an extra sturdy piece. Also, the fishing boats that the guides used weren't big enough for him, so most of the time he'd fish from the water's edge in an oversized armchair."

The night I stayed at the hotel, I was informed that fishermen could still have their lunches packed by the kitchen staff. They also mentioned that, if I ate in the dining room, I should top my meal off with a piece of Elaine Fitzgerald's banana cream pie.

After all these years, the hotel is still popular, and many of the repeat guests book a year in advance. This enables them to be sure of a reservation in this quaint historic setting the following year.

Cabin cruiser entering the locks at Jones Falls.

Photograph: Brian Morin /Parks Canada

The last remaining blacksmith shop on the Rideau Canal is at Jones Falls.

Photograph: Brian Morin /Parks Canada

The swinging lady has graced the corner of Eglinton and Victoria Park
Avenues in Toronto since 1962. This photograph was taken in December
1994.

LADY ON THE SWING

On any given day you'll find her at the corner of Toronto's Eglinton and Victoria Park Avenues. She's very pretty and always appropriately dressed for the season. Day in and day out, no matter the weather, the lady swings from the oldest activated billboard in the city. She was the brainchild of Paul Willison, when he swung his dealership over from Ford to Chrysler. When Global producer Lawrence Jackson suggested that perhaps she'd make a good story, she was already thirty-two years old. At that point she'd swung backwards and forwards for almost twelve thousand days.

Powered by a quarter-horsepower electric motor, she's rarely had a sick day. She's never been christened with a real name and has always gone by "the lady," "the gal" or "the princess on the swing." Even after Mr. Willison's passing in September of '93, the Chrysler showplace still retains the sign. Paul's nephew, Michael Tappenden, president of the dealership, said, "No matter what we do, spend thousands on advertising or build the largest Chrysler showroom in Canada, nothing seems to matter. The public tells us the real reason they're here is his lady on the swing."

The ten-foot-tall cutout of a woman is actually a triplet. She's got two almost identical sisters waiting in the wings at the Etobicoke paint studio of Mediacom. I made arrangements with the sign company to show a few scenes of the artists at work. The Willison sign is made of metal and was being worked on by pictorial sign painters John Daniel and Jimmy Thompson. They're the last of a dying breed, because billboards today are made of non-rusting, non-ripping superflex and are painted by a computer. John began his career forty-three years ago in the English city of Leeds, Yorkshire. "I've painted this board two or three times a year," he said, "that adds up a little bit. We used to change the sign four times a year there was a lady for each season, but now we're down to three." Up on the scaffold, Jimmy Thompson was painting the lettering on the huge billboard. Before coming to Canada, Jimmy was a textile designer in Belfast, Northern Ireland.

Two weeks after I'd been out to Mediacom's paint studio, I met up with the four-man crew changing the sign. The summer lady, dressed in her bathing suit, was already on the ground, patiently waiting for her ride back to the warmth of the plant in Etobicoke. Her sister, wearing a cozy sweater and slacks, was being hoisted into place.

The winter of '85 was an exciting time at Willison's because the lady on the swing went missing. A one thousand-dollar reward was offered for her kidnappers. She was eventually discovered buried under a snowbank eighty feet from the sign; she'd blown off during a severe snowstorm. The reward money was donated to the Salvation Army's new Scarborough Grace Hospital.

Over the decades the dealership has have received many letters:

"Dear Sirs: Don't you think the time has come to change your billboard? Spring, summer, fall and winter . . . the girl swinging . . . year in and year out . . . I am sure she's lost her effectiveness. Surely your public relations people can come up with something new."

That letter was written in June of 1967.

A couple of days after my story went to air, Amy Ruddell, a Centennial College student on a Global internship program, stopped me in the hall to tell me that she liked the story. It had brought back childhood memories for her. When she was with her parents in the car, she'd always ask them to take her by the billboard, because she wanted to see how the lady on the swing was dressed.

ABOUT THE AUTHOR

Terry Culbert is Global Television's first one-man band. As a cameraman/reporter, he travels the entire province producing his own lifestyle and human interest stories. Raised of farm stock in the Irish-Canadian village of Lucan, Ontario, Terry began his career in television news at the age of eighteen, working for CFPL Television in London. At age thirty, he moved to Toronto, joining the CBC. In October of 1979, Terry joined the Global Television Network.

Photograph: Bob McAdorey

Cameraman Culbert in Irvine, Scotland

Photograph: Doug McLellan

Reporter Culbert in Wallaceburg, Ontario

For More Copies of

COUNTY ROADS

send $19.95 plus $4.50 to cover
GST, shipping and handling to:

GENERAL STORE PUBLISHING
1 Main Street, Burnstown, Ontario
K0J 1G0

Telephone 1-800-465-6072
Fax 613-432-7184

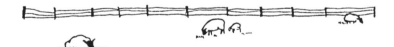